Black Historical Figures

SPORTS

Copyright © 2022 by Every Dollar Countz LLC
All rights reserved. This book or any portion thereof
may not be reproduced or used in any manner whatsoever
without the express written permission of the publisher
except for the use of brief quotations in a book review.

TABLE OF CONTENTS

171 SIMONE BILES

123 WILMA RUDOLPH

19 MUHAMMAD ALI

3 Charles Sifford	67 Vincent Jackson	131 Usain Bolt
11 Kareem Abdul Jabbar	75 Lebron James	139 Earl Lloyd
19 Muhammad Ali	83 Tiger Woods	147 Tony Dungy
27 Althea Gibson	91 Serena Williams	155 Candace Parker
35 Jackie Robinson	99 James Brown	163 Shani Davis
43 Jesse Owens	107 Hank Aaron	171 Simone Biles
51 Arthur Ashe	115 Michael Jordan	179 Cullen Jones
59 Jackie Joyner Kersee	123 Wilma Rudolph	187 Debi Thomas
		195 Frank Robinson

These Workbooks are geared to intrigue, inspire and motivate you to want to learn more about these Black Historical Figures(BHFs) and others. Also to do more research on your own. We know this isn't all the history of these individuals. We want you to do some of the research also. We try to be as accurate as possible during our research. If there are some stories or questions that aren't as stated, please contact us at info@wegonnalearntoday.com.

Charles Sifford

Charles Sifford

June 2, 1922 – February 3, 2015
GOLF PLAYER

LEFT BLANK ON PURPOSE

Charles Sifford

Charles Sifford

Charles Sifford

Charles Sifford

Charles Sifford

Charles Sifford

Directions: read the bio below and answer the following questions.

Hi, my name is Charles Sifford. I was born on June 2, 1922, in Charlotte, NC. When I was 10, I started caddying for the Carolina Country Club in Charlotte. I would get to play before hours and on the days that the Club was closed. I joined the United Open Association Tour in 1948 and I won the Negro National Open six times. In 1960, a California lawsuit caused the PGA to strike the "Caucasian only" clause from its regulations and I became the first African American to receive an official PGA Approved Players card on a one-year basis. I was known as the Jackie Robinson of golf and I was the first African American to play fulltime on the PGA Tour. I was also the first African American to be inducted into the World Golf Hall of Fame.

1. What clause stop me for joining the PGA prior to 1960?
    A. Age
    B. Caucasian only
    C. Not good enough
2. What year did I join United Open Association?
    A. 1950
    B. 1948
    C. 1960
3. Who am I known as in golf?
    A. Muhammad Ali
    B. Jackie Robinson
    C. Wilt Chamberlain

Directions: Answer the questions, to solve the crossword puzzle. You can use the internet if you get stuck on any question.

Across

5) People consider Charles the _____ of Golf.
6) Charles was the first Black golfer to play on the once all-white _____
7) Charles served in a segregated _____ during World War II.
8) Charles won the PGA _____ Championship in 1975.

Down

1) Charles Sifford was the first Black golfer inducted into the World Golf _____.
2) Tiger Woods credited Sifford for _____ him and his love of the game.
3) Charles won the United Golf Association's National Negro Open six times, including _____ wins from 1952 through 1956.
4) Charles was never invited to play in the _____ tournament, which didn't invite black players until 1975.

Directions: The images and text form an accomplishment of Charlie. Write the **sentence** below or the right number sequence.

#3 PGA   #2 the   #8 Los Angeles

#1 TOUR   #4 won   #6 in

#5 1969   #7

Directions: Unscramble the words below about Charles. See if you can get the bonus word.

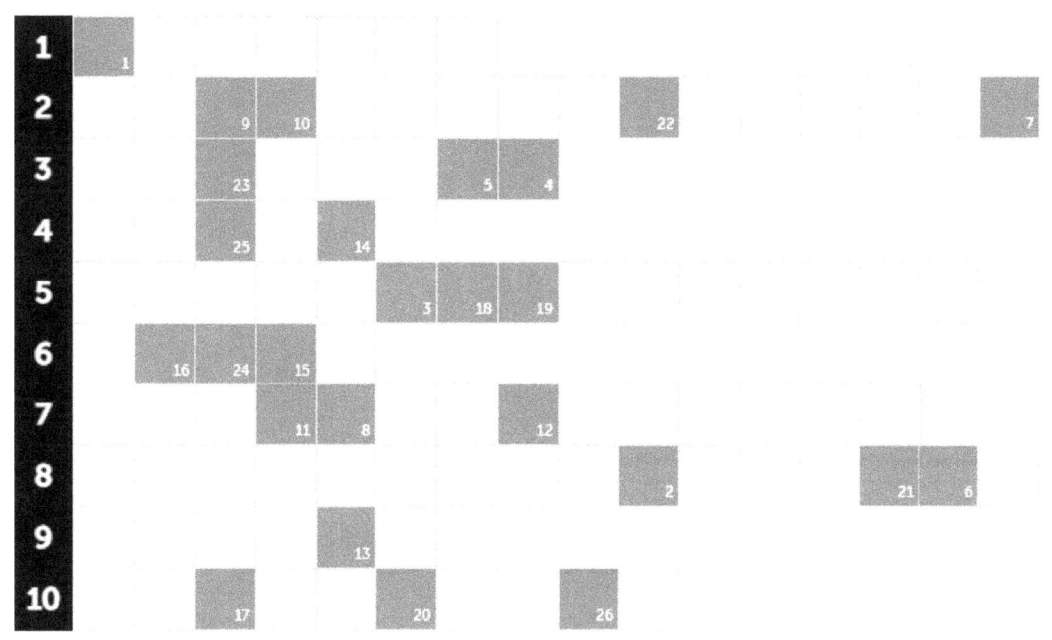

BONUS WORD

1 2 3 4 5 6 7 8 9 10 11 12 13 14 15 16 17 18 19

20 21 22 23 24 25 26

Unscramble Words

1) aoptgru
2) nneaponneitgrolao
3) joioeusl
4) spneuo
5) aliobawoanetfkt
6) yaddc
7) sennleosegpoal
8) ogtneafarrrprdheteo
9) ayrmus
10) ohfemlaalf

Directions: This is the WGLT Challenge. Solve the cryptogram. As the puzzle solver, you need to find which number belongs to which character. And this can be pretty challenging! You will need to match the number with the letter. There are some letters given to you below. This will help you solve the other words and unlock more characters. **Good Luck.**

Ferdinand Alcindor Jr.

Ferdinand Alcindor Jr.

April 16, 1947 – Present
BASKETBALL PLAYER

LEFT BLANK ON PURPOSE

Ferdinand Alcindor Jr

Ferdinand Alcindor Jr

Ferdinand Alcindor Jr

Ferdinand Alcindor Jr

Ferdinand Alcindor Jr

Ferdinand Alcindor Jr

Directions: read the bio below and answer the following questions.

Hi, my name is Ferdinand Alcindor Jr. I was born on April 16, 1947, in Harlem, NY. I graduated from Power Memorial Academy. I graduated from UCLA with a Bachelor of Arts in History. While I was a senior at UCLA, I converted to Islam and changed my name to Kareem Abdul-Jabbar, which means "noble one, servant of the Almighty." After graduation, I went into the NBA draft and was drafted as Number 1 by the Milwaukee Bucks in 1969. I won one Championship and three MVP Awards before requesting a trade. I was traded to the Los Angeles Lakers in 1975. I won five Championships and three more MVP Awards. One thing I was well known for was my trademark skyhook.

1. **What college did I go to?**
   A. UCLA
   B. Michigan
   C. Duke
2. **How many Championships ships did I win?**
   A. 5
   B. 6
   C. 3
3. **What is my trademark move?**
   A. Up and Under
   B. Double Clutch Shot
   C. Skyhook

Directions: Find the words associated with Kareem's life and career.

```
L O S A N G E L E S L A K E R S M J
U I E N A L P R I A J H X T Q N Y M
M M R X N M T R D S M B W L E Q H R
J S Q U C T J C C Q R O G H B W O I
N K X D G W H N I U J O C Q X O W M
T C P U Z U J I C I G J I Q K C U W
Q U O A U J W E R G A E S I N S R U
O B C U H L J L T N K E T L V Z Y
N E M O Z E Z E H R Y O E I E S H K
M E T O E L S D Y H F T M J S Z T R
C K Q O D J C R O T Y N H Q D D U O
B U P Z R G L O H T O R F R T Q E M
C A L Z T F K E Q B Z G O H E U H H
Y W T O A A Y J G V A U L F U E C O
P L R K I E J N V O S P V J E Z Z I
Q I F P A U C L A A V F Q N L P C R
M M T R Y N O E P A G C F H G A F P
E J U W Z G B N K D R S U N O Z P H
```

Find These Words

SKYHOOK
LOSANGELESLAKERS
THIRTYTHREE
BRUCELEE

MILWAUKEEBUCKS
ROOKIEOFTHEYEAR
GOGGLES

UCLA
MUSLIM
AIRPLANE

Directions: The images and text say something that Kareem is. Write the **sentence** below or the right number sequence.

#3    #9    #8 The

#2 all   #7    #6 of

#4 most   #5 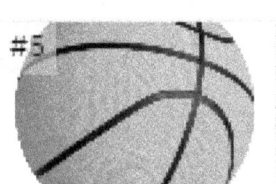   #1

Directions: Read and answer the questions below. There are clues in the puzzle to help you. Try and solve the cryptic message.

Clue for cryptic message: Kareem is known for this.

Questions

1) Kareem was the first _____ award winner.
2) Kareem got the _____ "The Tower from Power" in high school.
3) Kareem Arabic name means "the noble one, servant of the ____".
4) Kareem co-authored a mystery novel called Mycroft _____.
5) Bruce Lee and I were in the _____ Game of Death.
6) Kareem could have played for the Harlem _____.
7) Kareem use to play for the Milwaukee _____.

Directions: This is the WGLT Challenge. Solve the cryptogram. As the puzzle solver, you need to find which number belongs to which character. And this can be pretty challenging! You will need to match the number with the letter. There are some letters given to you below. This will help you solve the other words and unlock more characters. **Good Luck.**

Cassius Marcellus Clay Jr.

Cassius Marcellus Clay Jr.

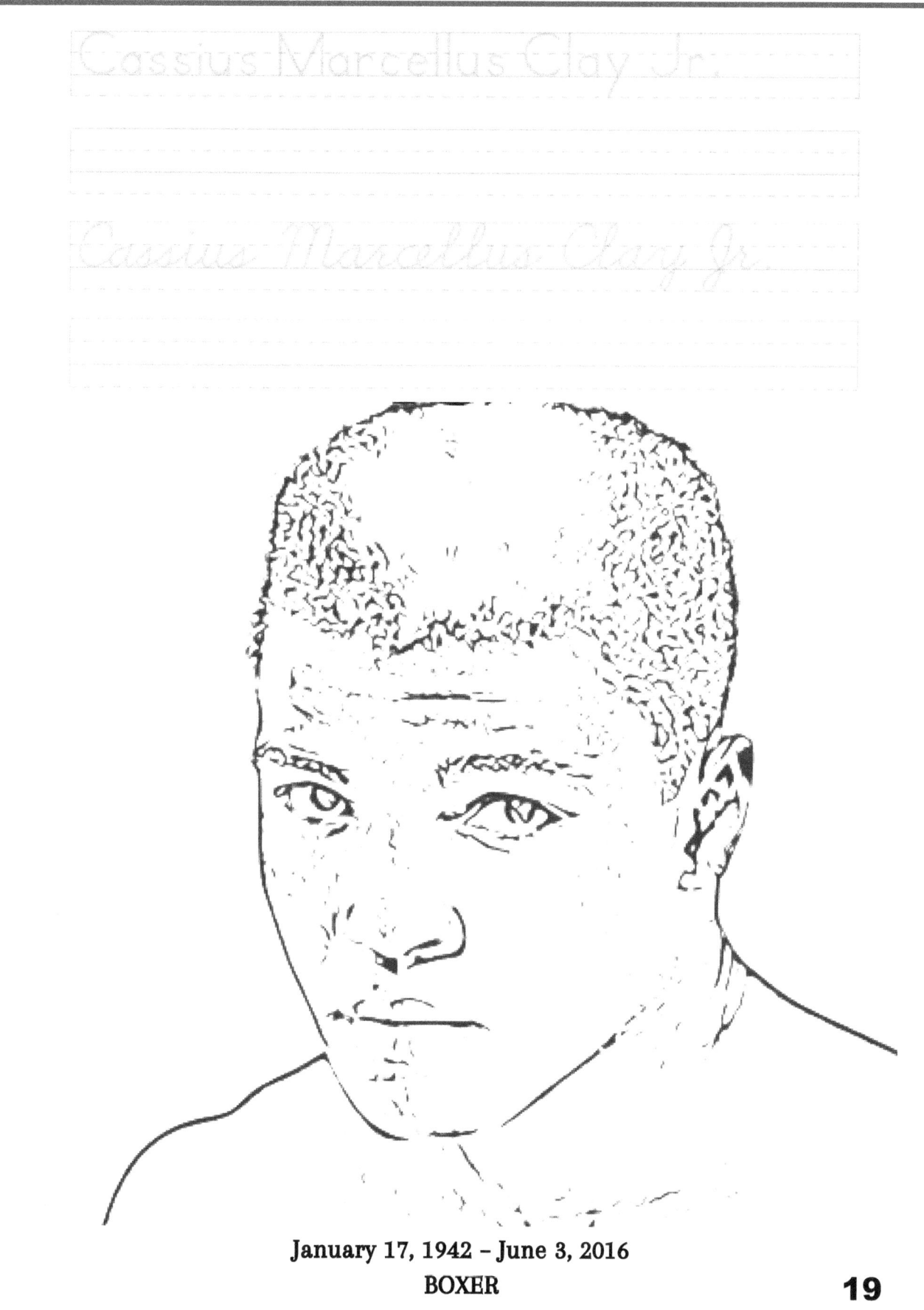

January 17, 1942 – June 3, 2016
BOXER

LEFT BLANK ON PURPOSE

Cassius Marcellus Clay Jr.

Cassius Marcellus Clay Jr.

Cassius Marcellus Clay Jr.

Cassius Marcellus Clay Jr.

Cassius Marcellus Clay Jr.

Cassius Marcellus Clay Jr.

Directions: read the bio below and answer the following questions.

Hi, my name is c Marcellus Clay Jr. I was born on January 17, 1942, in Louisville, KY. I attended Central High School. In 1954, at the age of 12, I started my amateur boxing career with a win off a split decision. I won the light heavyweight gold medal in the 1960 Summer Olympics in Rome. My amateur record was one hundred wins and five losses. I started my professional career in 1960. I went on a winning streak for the next three years: 19-0 and 15 knockouts. That next year, I won the heavyweight championship by beating Sonny Liston in seven rounds with a TKO. Not too long after this, I changed my name to "Cassius X" and then to "Muhammad Ali" after converting fully to Islam. One thing I'm known for is being known as "The Greatest." When people asked me why I was The Greatest, I told them, "I'm the most talked about, most publicized, the most famous and the most colorful fighter in history. And I'm the fastest heavyweight with feet and hands who ever lived."

1. Who did I beat to become the Heavyweight Champion?
    A. Joe Frazier
    B. Zbigniew Pietrzykowski
    C. Sonny Liston
2. What year did I become a Pro Boxer?
    A. 1954
    B. 1960
    C. 1963
3. What am I known as?
    A. Baptists
    B. The Greatest
    C. Singer

Directions: Answer the questions, to solve the crossword puzzle. You can use the internet if you get stuck on any question.

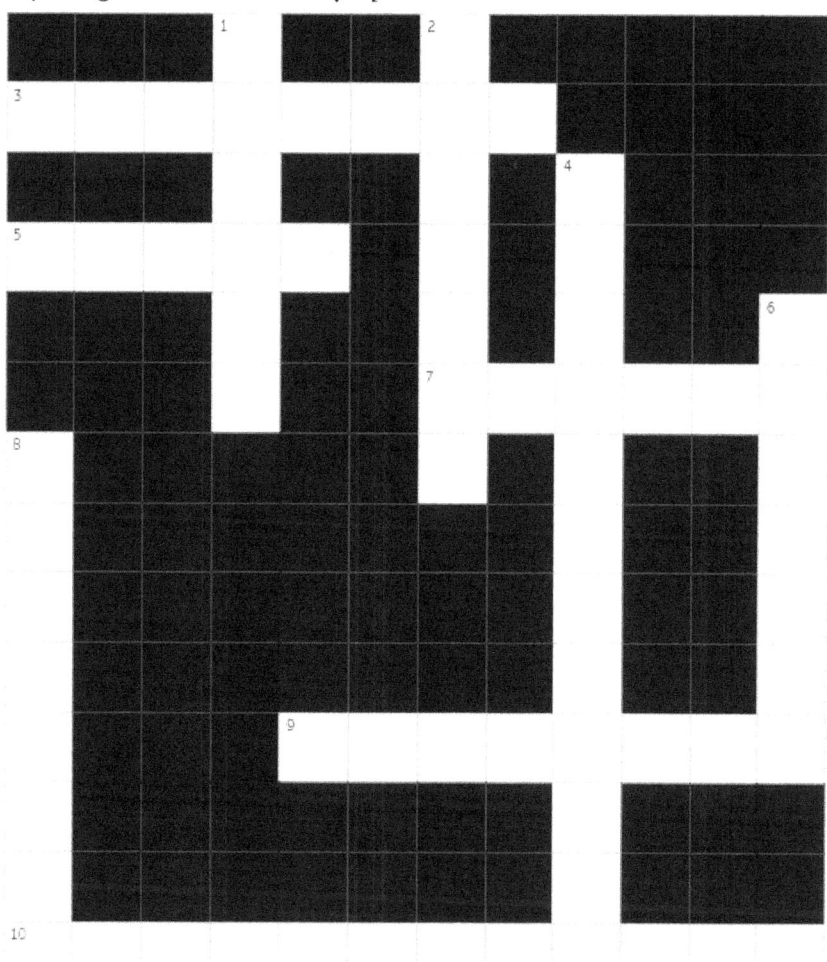

Across

3) In 1963, Muhammad Ali and _____ Records released a spoken word album called "I Am the Greatest".
5) One of Ali's nicknames is "The People's _____".
7) The "Rumble in the Jungle," was fought in _____ at four in the morning.
9) Muhammad Ali went to President _____ White House dinner.
10) Cassius Clay's named came from a white _____.

Down

1) In the 1960 _____ Olympics, Muhammad Ali won the light heavyweight gold medal.
2) Muhammad Ali refused to serve in the U.S. Military to fight in the _____ War.
4) Muhammad Ali had sixty-one fights and knocked out _____ contenders.
6) My name was _____ X. before becoming Muhammad Ali.
8) Muhammad Ali suffered from _____.

Directions: The images and text form an fight of Muhammad Ali . Write the **sentence** below or the right number sequence.

#3

#5 in

#4 The

#2 the

#1 RUMBLE

Directions: Unscramble the words below about Charles. See if you can get the bonus word.

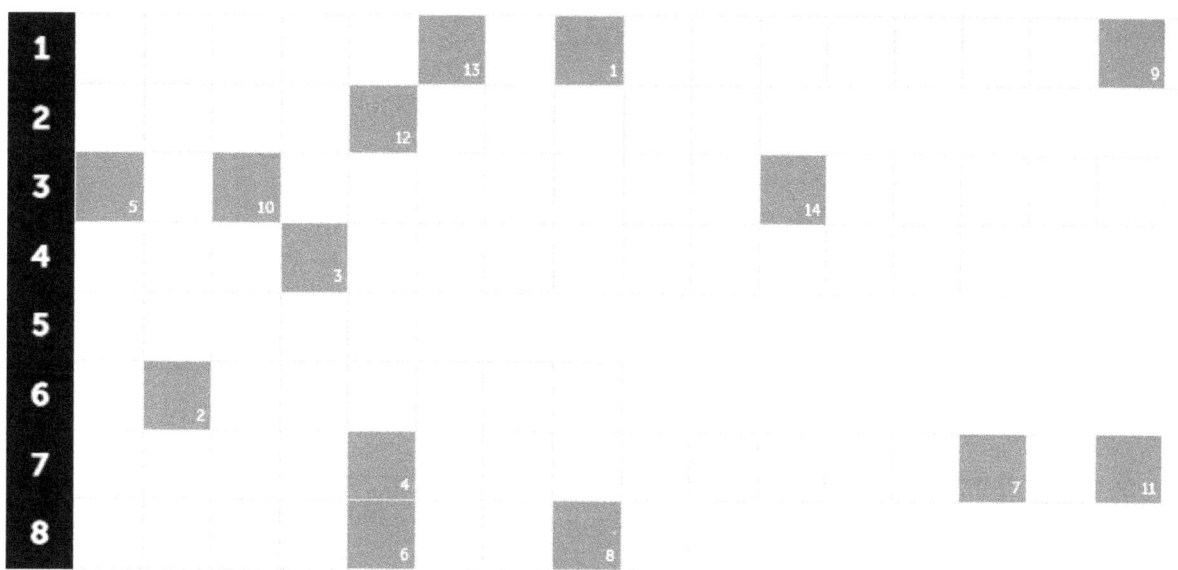

BONUS WORD

1 2 3 4 5 6 7 8 9 10 11 12 13 14

Unscramble Words

1) pbnxerflesoaioros 2) rodspnowke
3) mtghvihcayaephwe 4) umosecplmrsmiy
5) samll 6) MaolXlcm
7) evheiiggtwhahlty 8) sorkwdope

Directions: This is the WGLT Challenge. Solve the cryptogram. As the puzzle solver, you need to find which number belongs to which character. And this can be pretty challenging! You will need to match the number with the letter. There are some letters given to you below. This will help you solve the other words and unlock more characters. **Good Luck.**

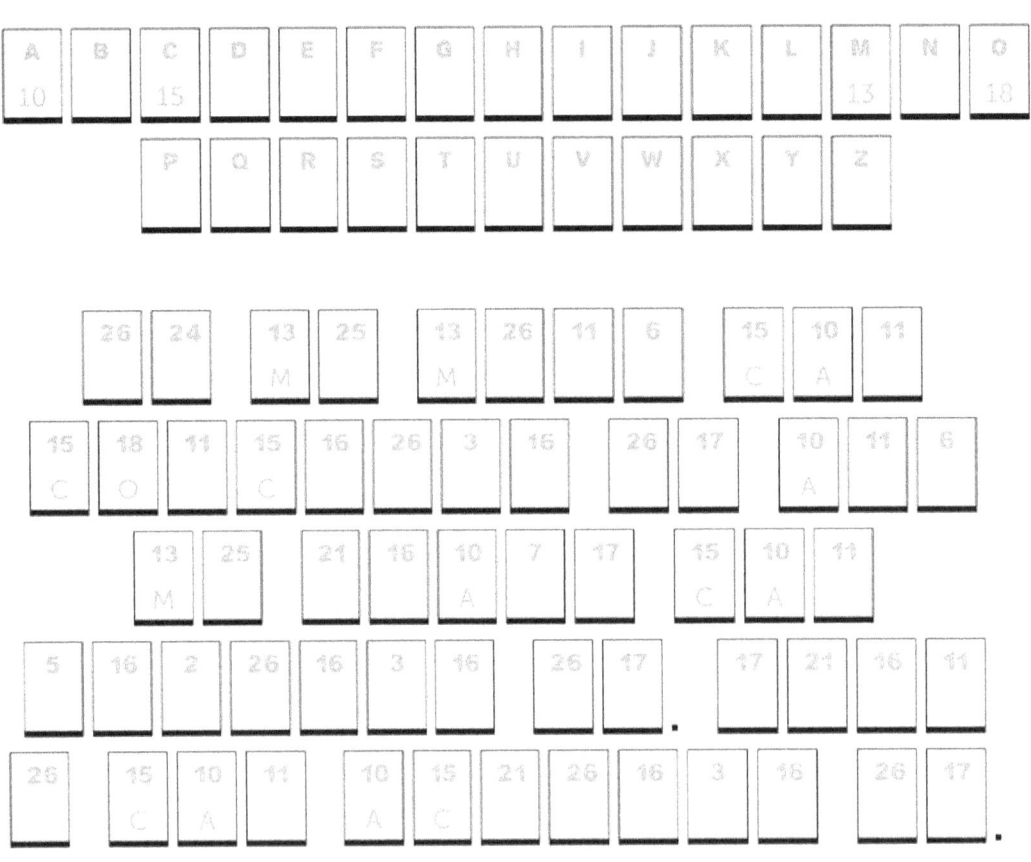

August 25, 1927 – September 28, 2003
TENNIS PLAYER

LEFT BLANK ON PURPOSE

Althea Gibson

Althea Gibson

Althea Gibson

Althea Gibson

Althea Gibson

Althea Gibson

Directions: read the bio below and answer the following questions.

Hi, my name is Althea Gibson. I was born on August 25, 1927, in the town of Silver in Clarendon County, SC. In 1930, my family and I moved to Harlem, NY, during the Great Migration. I took to paddle tennis at an early age. By 12, I was the NY City women's paddle tennis champion. In 1940, my neighbors paid for a junior membership and lessons at the Cosmopolitan Tennis Club for me. By 1941, I won my first tournament: the American Tennis Association (ATA) New York State Championship. I won the ATA national championship in the women's division in 1944 and 1945. In 1949, I became the first Black woman to play in the United States Lawn Tennis Association (USLTA) championships. The next year, I entered Florida AGM University (FAMU) on a full athletic scholarship and became a member of the Alpha Kappa Alpha (AKA) sorority. In 1950, I became the first Black player to receive an invitation to the Nationals.

1. What college did I go to?
   A. Tougaloo College
   B. Florida A&M University
   C. Clark University
2. What year did I participate in Nationals?
   A. 1952
   B. 1950
   C. 1949
3. What age did I become NY City Women paddle tennis champ?
   A. 15
   B. 23
   C. 12

Directions: Find the words associated with Althea's life and career.

```
H A J J T Y O V K Q T K O X E H N C
K D G K T G Y K I N E B G T E N G D
K Q K Y W R E T T O R T E B O L G D
Y Z I Y L R K C V Q V C J X C A U R
L R E I H L E D W E N K T U Y T M K
J Z K D X N W Y S C D I L O O V A L
T J D T N Q U V V Y K P N O U F K W
G K X Q E C N Y G D N B I D I F U F
V J K X P M S H K J R O S V V Z T A
M C W Y O C I Y F A N A D Y V Z D C
Y E G E H I N O F N Y E E E T M U O
U Y U L C X N V I J H A P N L M H G
G L T M N C E C B P H W C O W B Q U
H O Z T E T T N R P V K U I . L I G
M N F T R K D W X I H R Z I A S O W
D C J L F L I O R O M E R H M M . N
B C L E O R D B G B O E F U P N A U
A C K X Y G K X S P C U V X P V M J
```

Find These Words

WIBLEDON   FRENCHOPEN   U.S.OPEN
GOLF   TENNIS   GLOBETROTTER
JAMAICA   ROME   NEWDELHI
CEYLON

Directions: The images and text form an accomplishment of Althea. Write the **sentence** below or the right number sequence.

#10  #9  #3

#8 1958   #5    #1 the

#7 Female   #2 of   #6 In

#11 and   #12    #4 was

Directions: Read and answer the questions below. These are the different forms of poetry. There are clues in the puzzle to help you. Try and solve the cryptic message.

Clue for cryptic message: Althea made history when this happened.

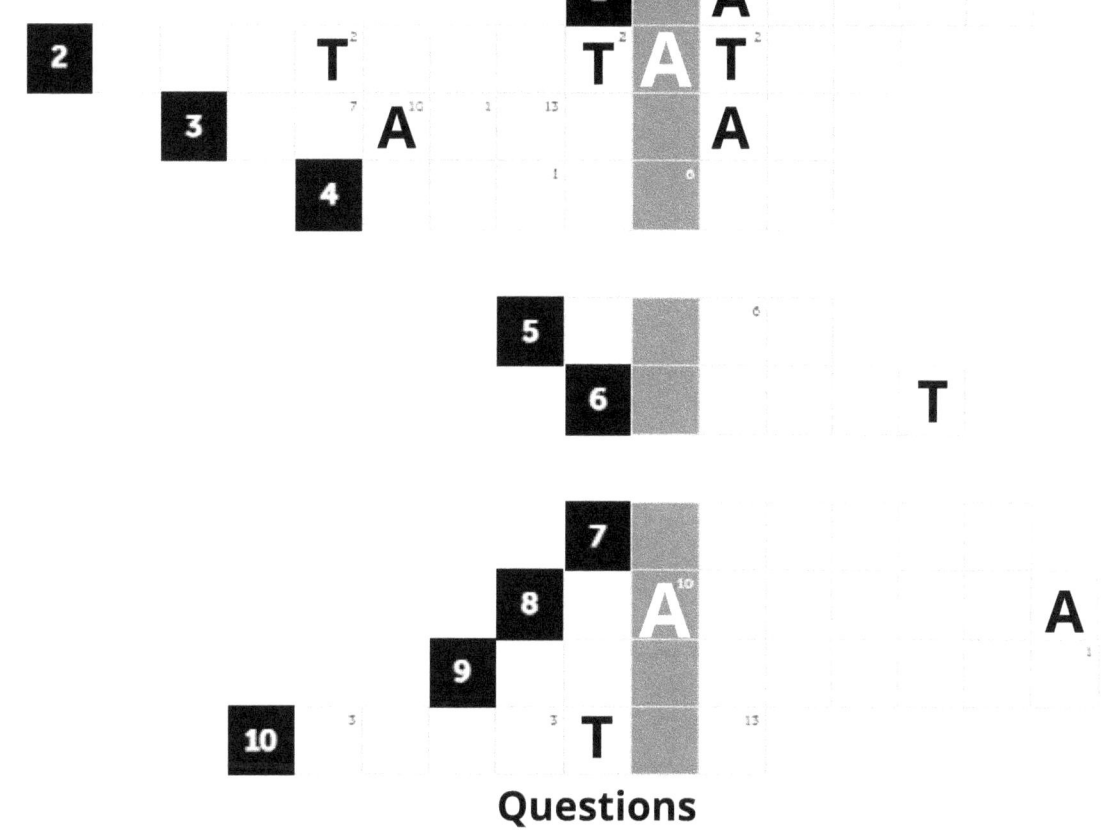

Questions

1) Althea use to play a series of exhibition matches against Karol Fageros before _____ Globetrotter basketball games.

2) Althea was the first black player to win ____ Open.

3) In 1956, Althea Gibson became the first African-American athlete to win a _____ tournament

4) In 1960, Althea won the ____ title.

5) Althea was the first African-American competitor on the women's pro ____ tour

6) Althea was the _____ champion to receive the Wimbledon trophy personally from Queen Elizabeth II.

7) Althea was the first black player to win _____ Open.

8) In 1951, Althea Gibson won her first international title, the _____ Championships in Jamaica,

9) Althea was the first black player to win _____.

10) Althea was the first African-American ever _____ to play at Wimbledon.

33

Directions: This is the WGLT Challenge. Solve the cryptogram. As the puzzle solver, you need to find which number belongs to which character. And this can be pretty challenging! You will need to match the number with the letter. There are some letters given to you below. This will help you solve the other words and unlock more characters. **Good Luck.**

Jack Robinson

Jack Robinson

35

January 31, 1919 – October 24, 1972
BASEBALL PLAYER

LEFT BLANK ON PURPOSE

Jack Robinson

Jack Robinson

Jack Robinson

Jack Robinson

Jack Robinson

Jack Robinson

Directions: read the bio below and answer the following questions.

Hi, my name is Jack Roosevelt Robinson. I was born on January 31, 1919, in Cairo, GA. I went to John Muir High School. While there, I played varsity and lettered in basketball, football, track and baseball. I then attended Pasadena Junior College. I continued to participate in the same sports. I broke my brother Mack's broad-jump record by jumping 25 f.t and 6½ in. on May 7, 1938. That same year, I was elected to the All-Southland Junior College Baseball Team and was selected as the region's Most Valuable Player. After graduating from PJC in spring 1939, I enrolled at UCLA, where I became the school's first athlete to win varsity letters in four sports: baseball, basketball, football and track. I made my major league debut on April 15, 1947. In 1955, I won my only championship; my team, the Brooklyn Dodgers, beat the NY Yankees.

1. What sport didn't I play in UCLA?
   A. Track
   B. Lacrosse
   C. Baseball
2. What year did I win my championship with the Dodgers?
   A. 1950
   B. 1955
   C. 1946
3. I was the first athlete to do what at UCLA?
   A. Letter in four sports
   B. Win a championship
   C. Play all year long

Directions: Answer the questions, to solve the crossword puzzle. You can use the internet if you get stuck on any question.

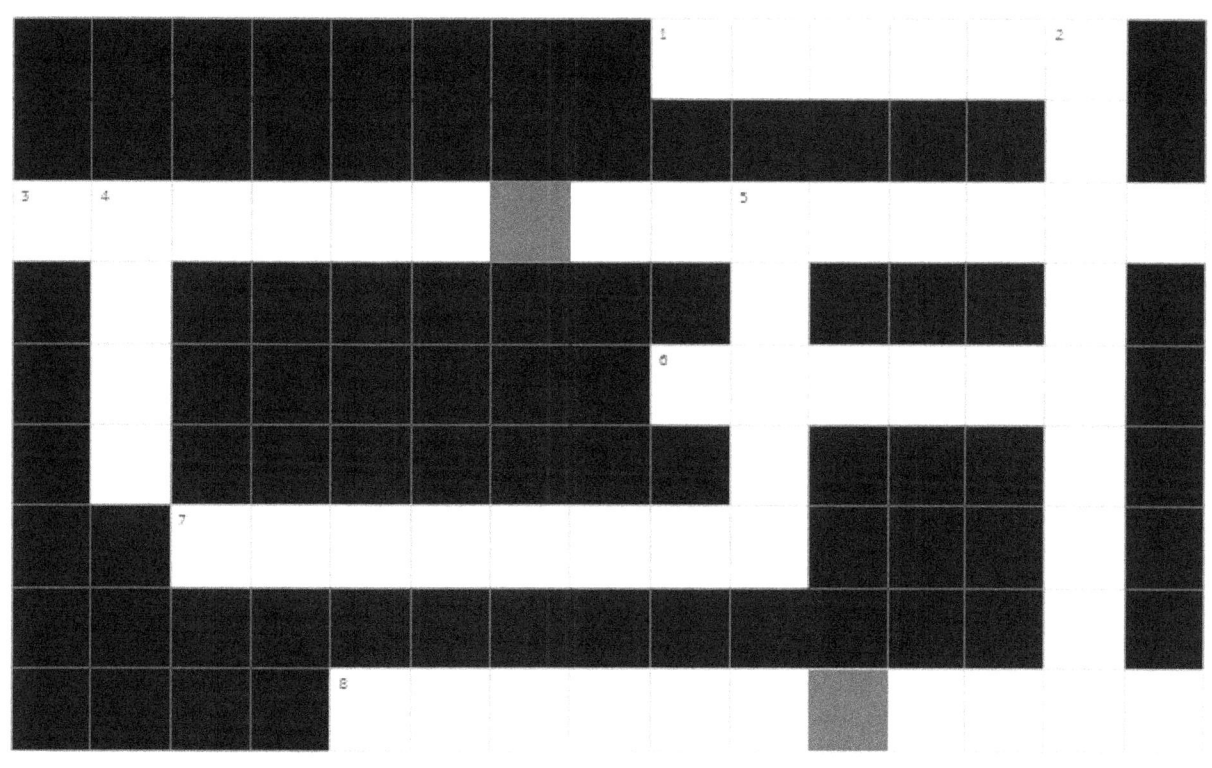

Across

1) While at UCLA, Jackie became the first student to ____ in four different sports in a single season.
3) Jackie played himself In the 1950 Hollywood film "The ___ ___ Story."
6) Jackie Robinson was 1947's ____ of the Year.
7) Jackie broke the Major League Baseball's color barrier in 1947 with the _____ Dodgers.
8) Jackie played for the ___ _____ Monarchs in the Negro National League.

Down

2) Jackie middle name came from President _____.
4) Jackie served in the U.S. ____ during World War II.
5) Jackie was good friends with Joe Luis aka "The ____ Bomber".

39

Directions: The images and text form an accomplishment of Jackie. Write the **sentence** below or the right number sequence.

#3

in

#7

#1    #6    #4   was

#2    #5

Directions: Unscramble the words below about Jack. See if you can get the bonus word.

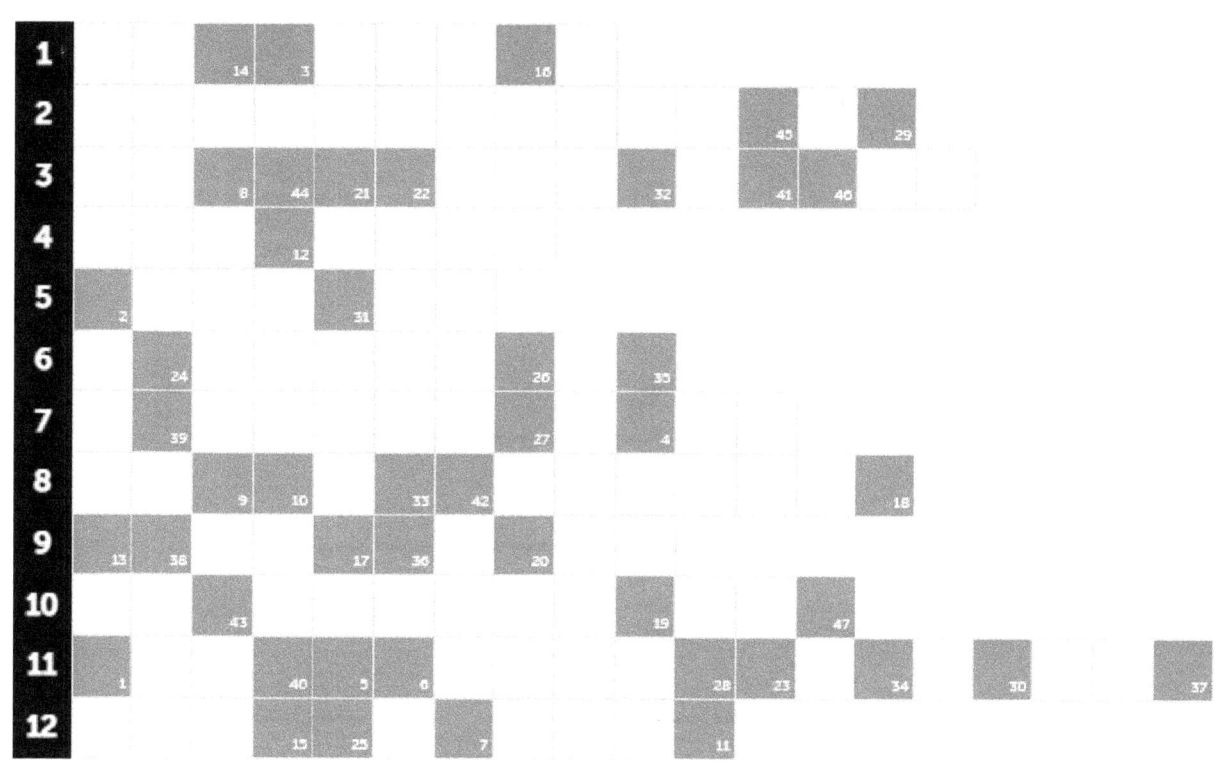

BONUS WORD

1 2 3 4 5 6 7 8 9 10 11 12 13 14 15 16 17

18 19 20 21 22 23 24 25 26 27 28 29 30 31 32 33 34 35 36

37 38 39 40 41 42 43 44 45 46 47

Unscramble Words

1) COuhclfol
2) rokosBdryDlgoe
3) oeeohtfoReiarYk
4) lblsaeba
5) rtSAall
6) lFaoemafHl
7) rnhrcikeycba
8) aleaRntrsolMyo
9) lrWdWolrla
10) aulHlonuBerso
11) bsSonaeoyriRktJnioc
12) sWheoBGugre

41

Directions: This is the WGLT Challenge. Solve the cryptogram. As the puzzle solver, you need to find which number belongs to which character. And this can be pretty challenging! You will need to match the number with the letter. There are some letters given to you below. This will help you solve the other words and unlock more characters. **Good Luck.**

James Cleveland Owens

September 12, 1913 – March 31, 1980
TRACK AND FIELD

43

LEFT BLANK ON PURPOSE

James Cleveland Owens

James Cleveland Owens

James Cleveland Owens

James Cleveland Owens

James Cleveland Owens

James Cleveland Owens

Directions: read the bio below and answer the following questions.

Hi, my name is James Cleveland Owens. I was born on September 12, 1913, in Oakville, AL. My family and I moved to Cleveland, OH during the Great Migration. When my new teacher asked me what my name was for her roll book, I said "J.C.," but because of my strong Southern accent, she thought I said "Jesse." The name stuck and now I'm known as Jesse Owens. I first came to national attention as a student of East Technical High School in Cleveland; I equaled the world record of 9.4 seconds in the 100-yard (91 m) dash and long-jumped 24 ft. 9½ in. (7.56 m) at the 1933 National High School Championship in Chicago. I went to Ohio State University, where I gain the nickname "Buckeye Bullet." I won eight individual NCAA championships from 1934–1935. In 1936, I participated in the Summer Olympics in Berlin. I competed in the 100 and 200 m dashes, the long jump and the 4x100 relay and won gold medals in every event.

1. Who did I get my nickname from?
   A. My mother
   B. My father
   C. My teacher
2. How many gold medals did I win in Summer Olympics?
   A. 1
   B. 3
   C. 4
3. What college did I go to?
   A. The Ohio State University
   B. Michigan University
   C. Alabama University

Directions: Find the words associated with Jesse's life and career.

```
C M G E O R G E W B U S H Y E Y S F
W Q G G N I I H G C K O X R U M V L
P L O T T P M I O K L O E U L K N M
X S S R J U E M Y T Z T P Y G E M
G F K L Z A N R M A U F B V J S J V
Q N B E A S C P B R Z W P U G W P T
P E U E M D I K O Q B V W F N F H P
E N C J M C E H - H I L F E D E E D
V Y K P S A D M O N X Y W K O Q B Z
B I E N N I F F D Q - Y G H B N T A
O D Y C K G X F O L O F I C A X Q D
D Z B R B S D V O U O O I Y T O F I
O P U Y I D G T R L S G V E Q L F D
N Z L V T N Q M Z T L T R X L C T A
V X L Z S I E T A C J A Z U D D X S
Z L E M M T R T A E X A H U O I I J
I B T R S T E G T R A T M D O F Z H
V N Y O B R P C Z F B E R L I N M Z
```

Find These Words

THEOHIOSTATE   BUCKEYBULLET   TRACK-N-FIELD
OLYMPICS   FOURGOLDMEDALS ADIDAS
NEWYOURMETS   BERLIN   GEORGEWBUSH
HALLOFFAME

47

Directions: The images and text form an accomplishment of Jesse. Write the **sentence** below or the right number sequence.

#2 name

#4 is   #1

#6 My

Directions: Read and answer the questions below. There are clues in the puzzle to help you. Try and solve the cryptic message.

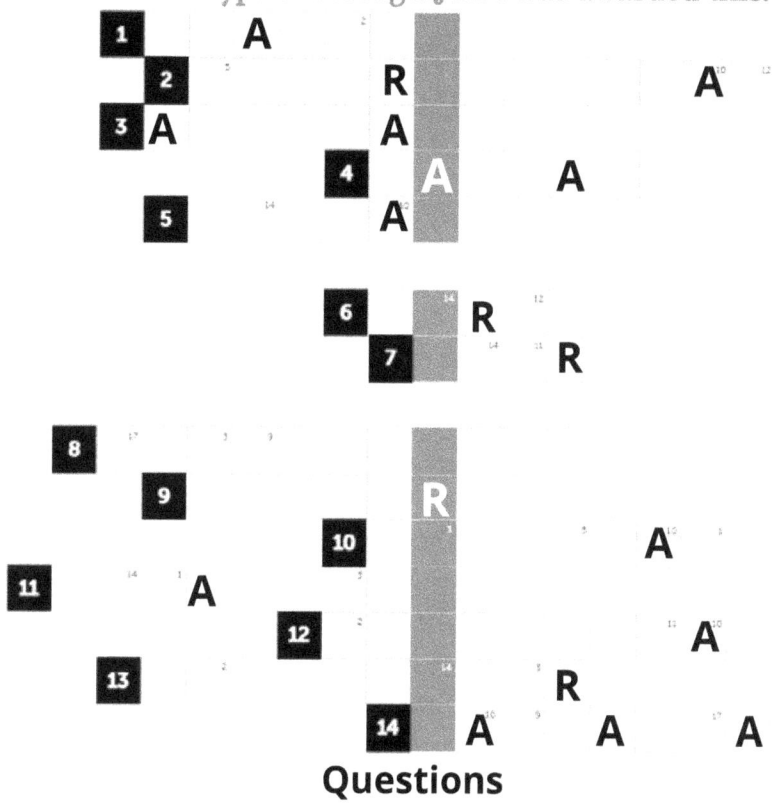

Questions

1) The Ohio State Department of Athletics added a 10,000-seat track and field _____ in his name.
2) Jesse Owens was posthumously awarded the _____ Gold Medal by President George H. W. Bush.
3) The Jesse Owens Award is USA Track and Field's highest _____ for the year's best track and field athlete.
4) Jesse was the first black man to be _____ of an Ohio State Varsity team.
5) The United States _____ Service issued two postage stamps in his honor.
6) 1935 is remembered as the day when Jesse Owens established four _____ records in athletics.
7) Jesse Owens won _____ gold medals in the 1936 Olympics
8) Jesse set a world record in the long jump that stood for _____ years straight without being broken.
9) Jesse Owens college coach was Larry _____.
10) Jesse Owens helped form a baseball league by the name of, the _____ Negro Baseball League
11) Jesse Owens inspired Carl Lewis who won four gold medals in the _____ Olympics in 1984.
12) Jesse won a record eight _____ NCAA championships
13) In 1955, President _____ enlisted Jesse as a goodwill ambassador.
14) Jesse and his United States teammates sailed on the SS _____ to Berlin for the Olympics.

Directions: This is the WGLT Challenge. Solve the cryptogram. As the puzzle solver, you need to find which number belongs to which character. And this can be pretty challenging! You will need to match the number with the letter. There are some letters given to you below. This will help you solve the other words and unlock more characters. **Good Luck.**

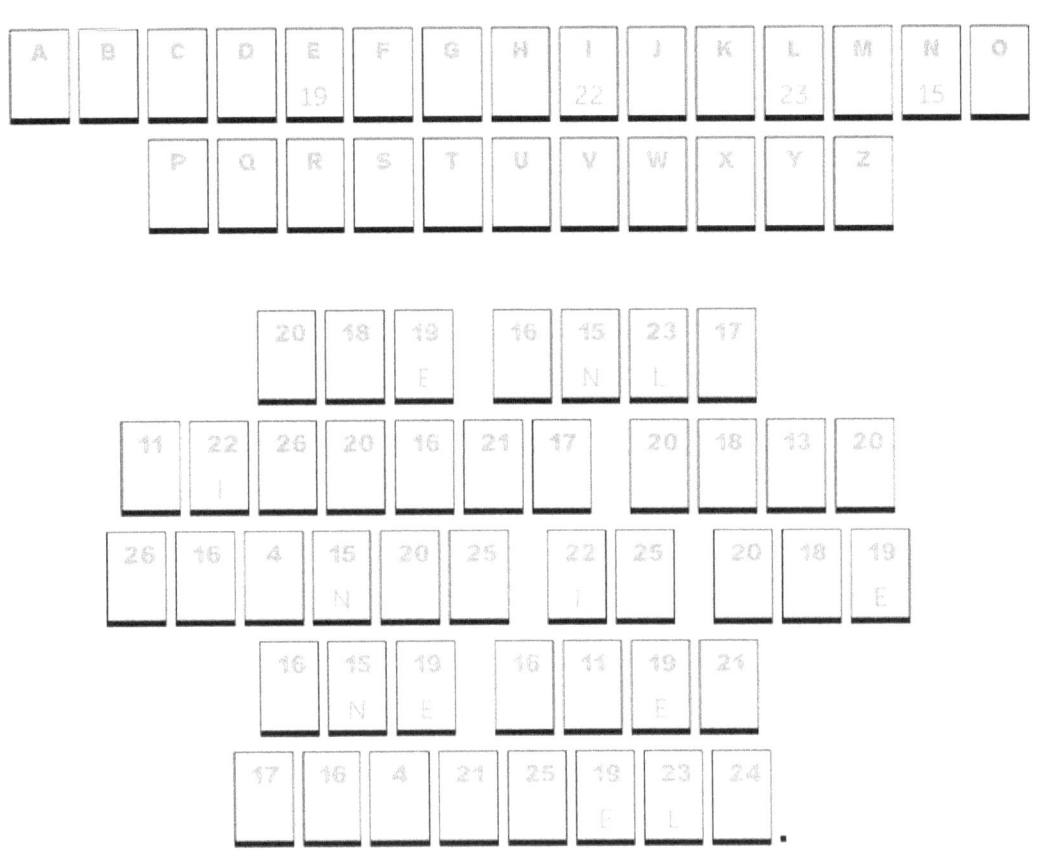

Arthur Ashe

51

July 10, 1943 – February 6, 1993
TENNIS PLAYER

Arthur Ashe

Arthur Ashe

Arthur Ashe

Arthur Ashe

Arthur Ashe

Arthur Ashe

Directions: read the bio below and answer the following questions.

Hi, my name is Arthur Robert Ashe Jr. I was born on July 10, 1943, in Richmond, VA. I was 6 when I started playing tennis. I graduated from Summer High School in St. Louis. I was the first African American to win the National Junior Indoor Tennis title, after which I was awarded a scholarship to UCLA in 1963. While at UCLA, I became a member of the Kappa Alpha Psi fraternity. I was also a member of the ROTC, so after I graduated from UCLA with a bachelor's degree in Business Administration, I joined the Army as a second lieutenant in the Adjutant General Corps. After leaving the military, I continued my professional tennis career. I won three Grand Slam singles titles. I was the first Black player to be selected for the United States Davis Cup team and was the only Black man ever to win the singles title at Wimbledon, the U.S. Open and the Australian Open.

1. How many Grand Slam singles titles did I win?
    A. 1
    B. 3
    C. 5
2. What College did I attend?
    A. Hampton University
    B. Fisk University
    C. UCLA
3. What fraternity am I apart of?
    A. Kappa Alpha Psi
    B. Alpha Phi Alpha
    C. Omega Psi Phi

Directions: Answer the questions, to solve the crossword puzzle. You can use the internet if you get stuck on any question.

Across
3) Arthur was the first African American to be _____ no 1 in the world.
4) In 1968, Arthur was the first black man to win the _____.
6) Arthur was the first African American man to be inducted into the International Tennis ___ ___ ___.
8) Arthur is the _____ African American male tennis player to win the U.S. Open and Wimbledon singles titles.

Down
1) Arthur won three ____ ____ single titles.
2) In 1975, Arthur was the first black man to win _____.
4) The new home for the _____ was named the Arthur Ashe Stadium.
5) Arthur was infected with an AIDS virus from a blood transfusion he had in 1983 while in a _____ surgery.
7) Arthur served in the U.S. _____ during the Vietnam War.

Directions: The images and text form an accomplishment of Arthur. Write the **sentence** below or the right number sequence.

#1 the

#4

#2

#9

#3

#8 was

#5

#7 a

#6 ARMY

Directions: Unscramble the words below about Arthur. See if you can get the bonus word.

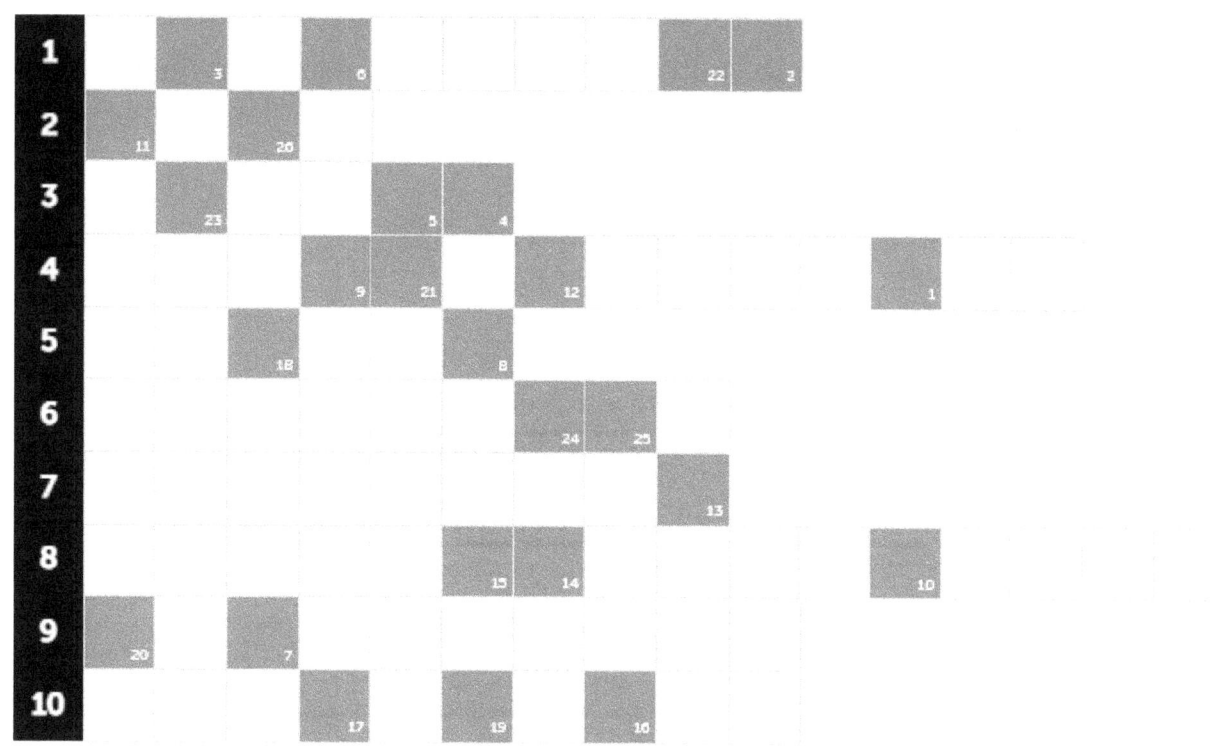

BONUS WORD

Unscramble Words

1) edrrdbuabe
2) mary
3) nsitne
4) ruinsteaplnaao
5) sonepu
6) wdnoelmib
7) gsnlaradm
8) littnrcodinsenpe
9) enfhpnrcoe
10) aohfllfaem

Directions: This is the WGLT Challenge. Solve the cryptogram. As the puzzle solver, you need to find which number belongs to which character. And this can be pretty challenging! You will need to match the number with the letter. There are some letters given to you below. This will help you solve the other words and unlock more characters. **Good Luck.**

Jacqueline Joyner

Jacqueline Joyner

March 3, 1962 – Present
TRACK AND FIELD

Jacqueline Joyner

Jacqueline Joyner

Jacqueline Joyner

Jacqueline Joyner

Jacqueline Joyner

Jacqueline Joyner

Directions: read the bio below and answer the following questions.

Hi, my name is Jacqueline Joyner-Kersee. I was born on March 3, 1962, in East St. Louis, IL. I was named after Jacqueline Kennedy, the First Lady of the United States. I went to East St. Louis Lincoln Senior High School. During my senior year, I qualified for the finals in the long jump at the 1980 Olympic Trials and finished 8th. I went to UCLA, where I played both track and field and women's basketball. I won the Broderick Award as the nation's best female collegiate track and field competitor in 1983 and 1985. I won silver in the heptathlon for the 1984 Summer Olympics. In 1986, I became the first woman to score over 7,000 points in a heptathlon. At the 1988 Summer Olympics, I won gold medals in both the heptathlon and the long jump. I set the still-standing as of 2022 heptathlon world record of 7,291 points. At the 1992 Summer Olympics, I won gold again in the heptathlon and bronze in the long jump.

1. Who was I named after?
    A. My Grandmother
    B. The First Lady
    C. My Mother
2. What year did I set the heptathlon world record?
    A. 1984 Olympics
    B. 1992 Olympics
    C. 1988 Olympics
3. What did I win 2 gold medals in?
    A. Long Jump
    B. 100 meter dash
    C. Heptathlon

Directions: Find the words associated with Jackie's life and career.

```
K I A O R M K U B B G Q H L N P C Z
R I W L P V M U U W Q M S L V O I A
T Y B M Z N O T R J A H M C G V G
U F D M E M Q Y Y E K A L N P Q X D
R H D P O G R F N E L Z C C H E B V
D O S I O T A L C L S T T L U T R K
Z R E C W H D R O Y X R Y T V C E C
S J M S B C D F D V B O E H N H Z B
O E A B S Q F U Q N S T E J S R T P
F Z G P Q A E W U R O P R L E L R Y
T F L T M D C T X V T M A Q L H A H
B W L E Q Q T U F A F D H B E O T O
T D I O W D P L T J E L K C U K X D
R N W K U J M H M M P X K M I A P R
T D D M Y X L N D J N S A V V R A L
J C O F J O J L J T H X S W N R H S
J Z O I N E O T W A O F J U Q R K I
P H G L I G N T Z K P M U J G N O L
```

Find These Words

UCLA	OLYMPICS	HEPTATHLON
GOLDMEDALS	RICHMONDRAGE	LONGJUMP
GOODWILLGAMES	THEJERSEY	HALLOFFAME

63

Directions: The images and text form an accomplishment of Jackie's. Write the **sentence** below or the right number sequence.

#1 **Athlete**

#4 of

#2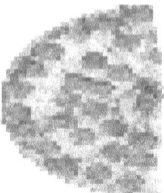

#7 of

#5

#3

#8 *Century*

#6 the

#11 the

#9

#10 **first**

Directions: Read and answer the questions below. These are the different forms of poetry. There are clues in the puzzle to help you. Try and solve the cryptic message.

Clue for cryptic message: Jackie was good at this.

Questions

1) Jackie won _____ Olympic gold medals.
2) Jackie was the first woman to _____ more than 7,000 points in the heptathlon event.
3) Jackie was the first African American woman to win an Olympic Medal in the _____.
4) Jackie was able to have overcome severe _____.
5) Jackie went to UCLA on a _____ scholarship
6) Sports Illustrated named her the _____ Female Athlete of the 20th Century.
7) Jackie wrote a book called A Woman's Place is _____.
8) Jackie won four gold medals at the _____ Championships.
9) Jackie was the first _____ to win back-to-back gold medals in the heptathlon.
10) Jackie was named after Jacqueline _____.

65

Directions: This is the WGLT Challenge. Solve the cryptogram. As the puzzle solver, you need to find which number belongs to which character. And this can be pretty challenging! You will need to match the number with the letter. There are some letters given to you below. This will help you solve the other words and unlock more characters. **Good Luck.**

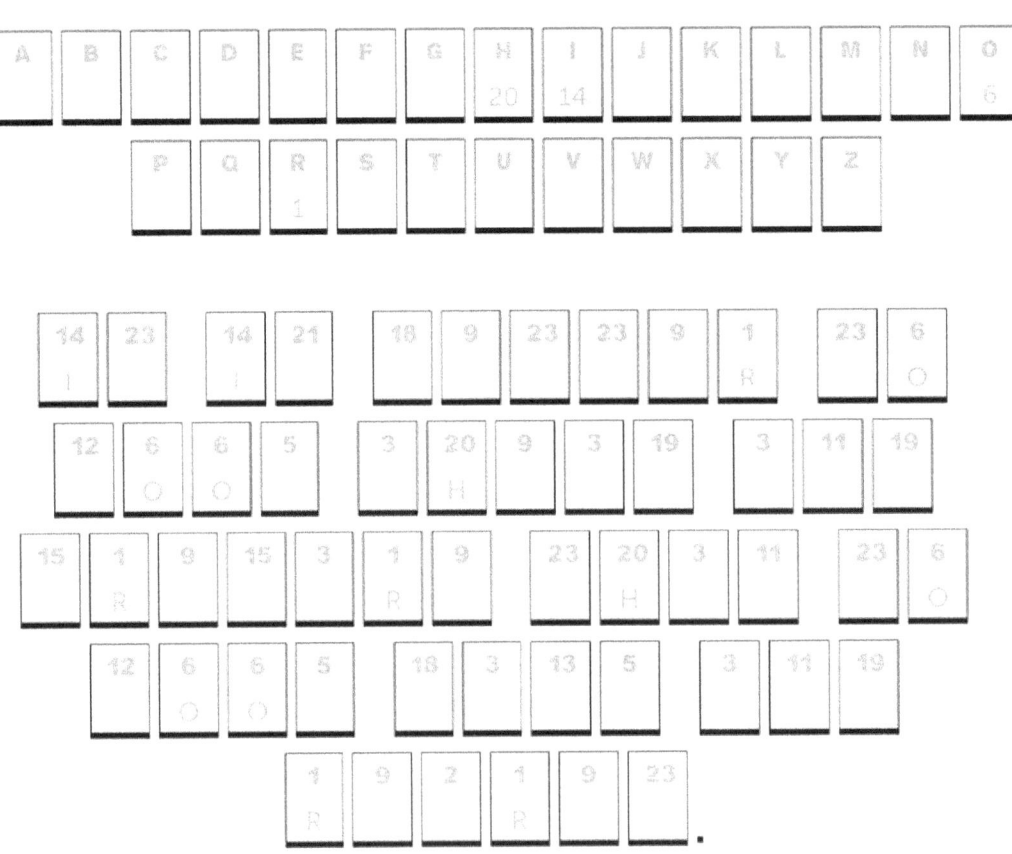

Vincent Edward Jackson

Vincent Edward Jackson

November 30, 1962 – Present
BASEBALL/FOOTBALL PLAYER

LEFT BLANK ON PURPOSE

Vincent Edward Jackson

Vincent Edward Jackson

Vincent Edward Jackson

Vincent Edward Jackson

Vincent Edward Jackson

Vincent Edward Jackson

Directions: read the bio below and answer the following questions.

Hi, my name is Vincent Edward Jackson I was born on November 30, 1962, in Bessemer, AL. When I was young, I constantly got into trouble, and my family described me as a "wild boar hog." They shortened this name by giving me the nickname "BO." I went to McCalla High School, where I played football and baseball and ran track. I was the two-time state champion in the decathlon. I also set the state school records for the indoor high jump and triple jump. I was selected by the NY Yankees in the second round but chose to attend Auburn University because I promised my mother that I would be the first in the family to go to a major college. I won the Heisman in 1985. I also won the Sugar Bowl and Liberty Bowl while at Auburn. I played professionally for the Kansas City Royals and the Los Angeles Raiders. I'm the only professional athlete in history to be named an All-Star in both baseball and football.

1. What sport didn't I do professionally?
    A. Track & Field
    B. Football
    C. Baseball
2. What year did I win the Heisman?
    A. 1982
    B. 1983
    C. 1985
3. What is my nickname?
    A. The Greatest
    B. BO
    C. The King

Directions: Answer the questions, to solve the crossword puzzle. You can use the internet if you get stuck on any question.

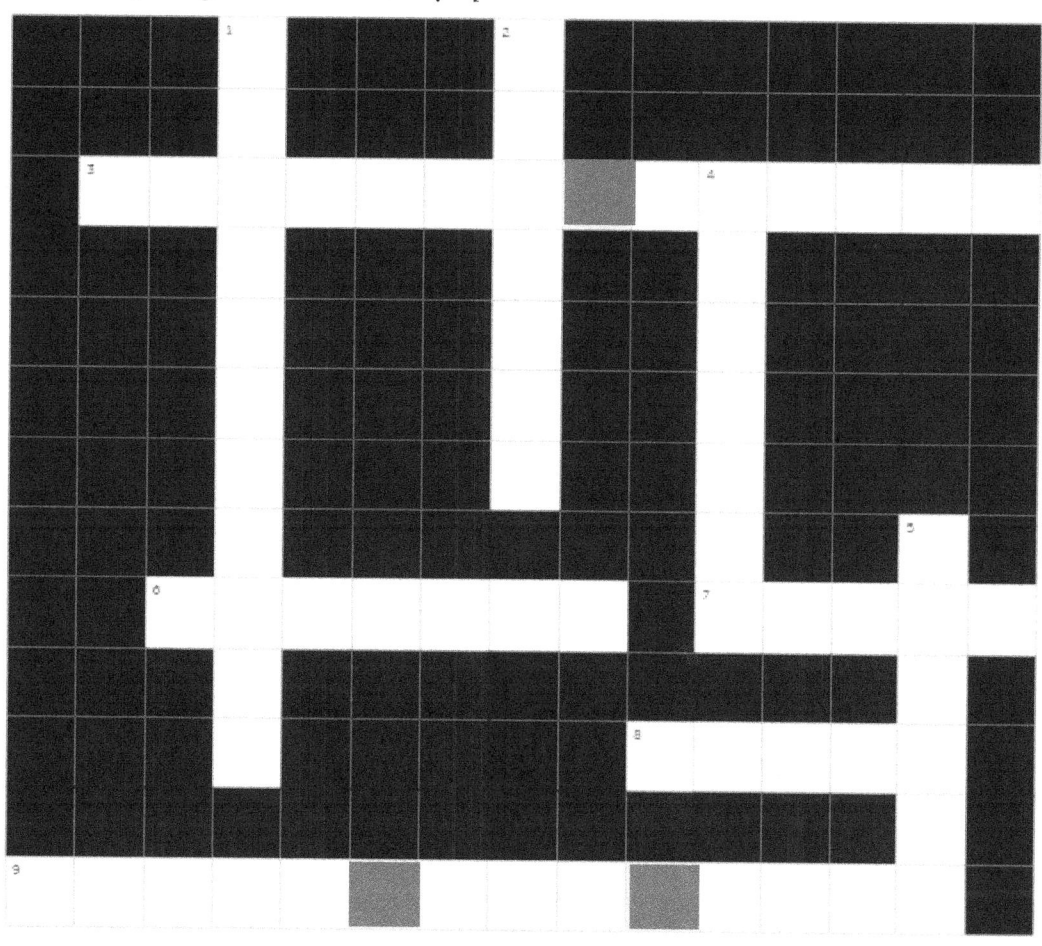

Across
3) Bo Jackson won the "_____ _____" while at Auburn University.
6) Bo was inducted into the _____ Football Hall of Fame in 1996.
7) Bo was named MVP after winning the _____ Bowl.
8) "Bo _____" was an advertising campaign by Nike.
9) Bo was the number one draft pick for the ___ ____ ____ in 1986, but refused to play for them.

Down
1) Auburn Tigers retired Bo's jersey number _____.
2) After High School, Bo turned down a deal with the New York _____.
4) Bo played for the Los Angeles _____ in the NFL.
5) Bo played for the _____ City Royals in the MLB.

Directions: The images and text form an accomplishment of Bo. Write the **sentence** below or the right number sequence.

#6  #7   #8 the   was   #10

#1    #9    #5

#4    #2 named   #3 and

#12 to   #11    #13 the

72

Directions: Unscramble the words below about Vincent. See if you can get the bonus word.

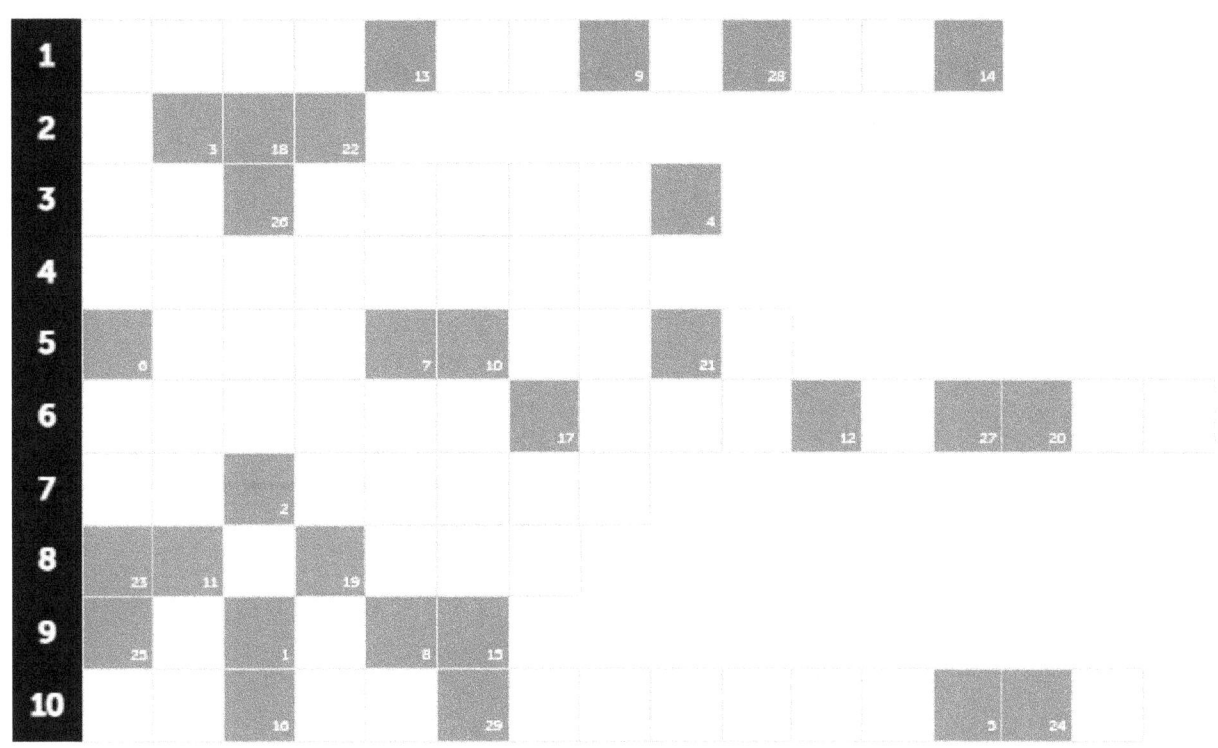

BONUS WORD

Unscramble Words

1) pneirhyoamsth
2) ikne
3) laerrsadi
4) sbalblea
5) haloealmff
6) asckyirsosntalha
7) llotfoab
8) nbookws
9) unarbu
10) ahthicegcxoiows

Directions: This is the WGLT Challenge. Solve the cryptogram. As the puzzle solver, you need to find which number belongs to which character. And this can be pretty challenging! You will need to match the number with the letter. There are some letters given to you below. This will help you solve the other words and unlock more characters. **Good Luck.**

LeBron Raymone James Sr.

LeBron Raymone James Sr.

December 30, 1984 – Present
BASKETBALL PLAYER

LeBron Raymone James Sr.

LeBron Raymone James Sr.

LeBron Raymone James Sr.

LeBron Raymone James Sr.

LeBron Raymone James Sr.

LeBron Raymone James Sr.

Directions: read the bio below and answer the following questions.

Hi, my name is LeBron Raymone James Sr. I was born on December 30, 1984, in Akron, OH. I went to St. Vincent-St. Mary High School and played football and basketball. My team and I won three division titles in four years. I went on to be drafted as Number 1 by the NBA draft for the Cleveland Cavaliers. I won NBA Rookie of the Year and became the first Cavalier to do that. I have won four NBA championships. One I won with the Cleveland Cavaliers, two with Miami Heat and one with the Los Angeles Lakers. I've won four Final MVPs and I'm the only player in NBA history to win that with three different franchises. I've also won four NBA MVPs and eighteen NBA All-Star appearances. I started the I Promise School in 2018 in Akron, OH. This school is supported by the LeBron James Family Foundation and specifically caters to at-risk children. Free tuition to the University of Akron for every graduating student is covered by the Akron I Promise Network Scholarship from the University of Akron, the LeBron James Family Foundation and JPMorgan Chase in 2015.

1. What team did I play for first?
    A. Miami Heat
    B. Los Angeles Lakers
    C. Cleveland Cavaliers
2. How many teams do I have NBA championships with?
    A. 1
    B. 4
    C. 3
3. What city was I born in?
    A. Youngstown
    B. Akron
    C. Fremont

Directions: Find the words associated with LeBron's life and career.

```
P T Q A K O W C H O S E N O N E P L
R A T K J F U G T L V F Y E B Q T U
L J O L Y M P I C S L Y J S A A W L
H Q I S K J L U U G O T L R S B O J
U N F I E K P H V B M I J E K Z W D
Q A D W C M G S U O V O Q K E V V Y
C T K Y V X A D Y E D Y X A T L U O
U Z Z R S Y N J R X B V T L B L R Z
C H A O O Y Q P G T D A Z S A V G K
R G M T W N O J B N E Z A E L G T V
A L R C H O - G X H I C S L L G X D
T Y V Z L Z D O I A S K Q E A Y O H
S F L F I Z C M H M M D S G D Y O K
- Y C K P G A Y O I T W T N Y A I I
L Y F O U I S I A U O M S A B F E U
L C V I M Q V E S T F K W S X H Q I
A W V K Y J T J Y U Z S B O C Q O L
C L E V E L A N D C A V A L I E R S
```

Find These Words

OLYMPICS ALL-STAR BASKETBALL
CLEVELANDCAVALIERS KINGJAMES LIVERPOOLFC
MIAMIHEAT CHOSENONE LOSANGELESLAKERS
AKRON-OHIO

Directions: The images and text form an accomplishment of LeBron's. Write the **sentence** below or the right number sequence.

#1

#8 is

in

#3

#4 considered

#2 the

#5 NBA #6

the

#7

1, 4, 3, 8, 5, 6, 2, 7

Directions: Read and answer the questions below. There are clues in the puzzle to help you. Try and solve the cryptic message.

Clue for cryptic message: LeBron's.

Questions

1) LeBron is a big New York _____ fan.
2) Lebron's started a school called "I _____ School".
3) LeBron is the _____ player to score 40 points in a game.
4) LeBron won an Olympic _____ Medal in 2008 and 2012
5) LeBron made the cover of Sports Illustrated as a high school _____.
6) LeBron was named to the first team all-state _____ team his sophomore year of high school
7) Lebron was the First Black Man on the Cover of Vogue _____ .
8) LeBron _____ Saturday Night Live in 2007.
9) One of LeBron's nicknames is "_____".

81

Directions: This is the WGLT Challenge. Solve the cryptogram. As the puzzle solver, you need to find which number belongs to which character. And this can be pretty challenging! You will need to match the number with the letter. There are some letters given to you below. This will help you solve the other words and unlock more characters. **Good Luck.**

Eldrick Tont Woods

Eldrick Tont Woods

December 30, 1975 – Present
GOLF PLAYER

Eldrick Tont Woods

Eldrick Tont Woods

Eldrick Tont Woods

Eldrick Tont Woods

Eldrick Tont Woods

Eldrick Tont Woods

Directions: read the bio below and answer the following questions.

Hi, my name is Eldrick Tont Woods. I was born on December 30, 1975, in Cypress, CA. I chose my nickname "Tiger" in honor of my father's friend, South Vietnamese Colonel Vuong Dang Phong, who had also been known as "Tiger." I started playing golf when I was 2 years old. When I was 8, I won the 9–10 boys' event at the Junior World Golf Championships. I went on to win that event six times. I went to Western High School and became the youngest U.S. Junior Amateur Champion. In 1994, I went on to win that event three consecutive times. I'm the only person that has won that event three times. I went to Stanford University. In 1996, I became the first golfer to win three consecutive U.S. Amateur titles and win the NCAA individual golf championship. I was only 20. I became a professional golfer after that. I'm tied for first in PGA Tour wins and I rank second in men's major championships with fifteen wins.

1. How old was I when I won my first event?
   A. 5
   B. 9
   C. 8
2. What year did I turn professional?
   A. 20
   B. 18
   C. 22
3. What college did I go to?
   A. Howard
   B. Fisk
   C. Stanford

Directions: Answer the questions, to solve the crossword puzzle. You can use the internet if you get stuck on any question.

Across

3) Tiger was _____ years old when he broke 80 on a golf course for the first time.
7) Tiger attended _____ University.
8) Tiger is the youngest golfer to win the career _____.

Down

1) Tiger was the world's first _____-dollar athlete.
2) Tiger has the most _____ ranked number one in golf with 683 almost the equivalent of 13 years.
4) Tiger is the only man to win the US _____ Championship three years in a row.
5) Tiger is a _____.
6) Tiger opened his first golf course in 2016, _____ National.

Directions: The images and text form an accomplishment of Tiger. Write the **sentence** below or the right number sequence.

#1 PLAYER

#2 [image]

#4 to

#3 WIN

#5 the

#6 the

#7 [image of golfer]

#8 is

#9 YOUNGEST

Directions: Unscramble the words below about Eldrick. See if you can get the bonus word.

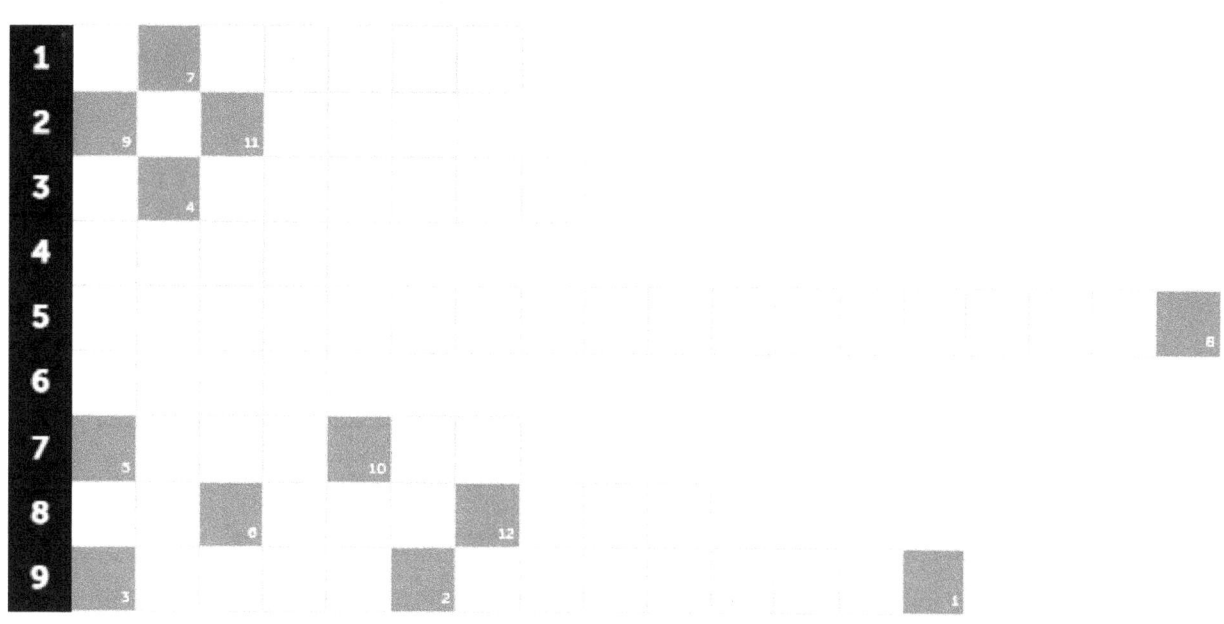

BONUS WORD

1 2 3 4 5 6 7 8 9 10 11 12

Unscramble Words

1) srastme
2) rlofge
3) iiesttlt
4) enik
5) siedunftosntrirvya
6) aotg
7) rupoatg
8) lmlahafoef
9) saeernohwcepee

Directions: This is the WGLT Challenge. Solve the cryptogram. As the puzzle solver, you need to find which number belongs to which character. And this can be pretty challenging! You will need to match the number with the letter. There are some letters given to you below. This will help you solve the other words and unlock more characters. **Good Luck.**

Serena Williams

Serena Williams

September 26, 1981 – Present
TENNIS PLAYER

LEFT BLANK ON PURPOSE

Serena Williams

Serena Williams

Serena Williams

Serena Williams

Serena Williams

Serena Williams

Directions: read the bio below and answer the following questions.

Hi, my name is Serena Williams. I was born on September 26, 1981, in Saginaw, MI. I started playing tennis at age 4. When I turned 10, my record was 46-3 on the U.S. Tennis Association junior tour and I was ranked first among players who were 10 and under. I started my professional career in 1995 at the Bell Challenge in Quebec. I was 15. By 2002, I was ranked number one with a 56-5 W/L record and eight singles titles. I was the first African-American to end a year with that ranking since Althea Gibson in 1958 and was the first woman to win three Grand Slam tournament titles in one year since Hingis in 1997. My three consecutive Grand Slam titles also made me the third player in tennis history to win the "Surface Slam," which was three Slam titles on three surfaces in the same calendar year. I have won 23 Grand Slam singles titles.

1. What year did I become a professional tennis player?
   A. 1997
   B. 1994
   C. 1995
2. What year did I first obtain the number 1 ranking?
   A. 2002
   B. 2000
   C. 2001
3. How many Grand Slams have I won?
   A. 24
   B. 21
   C. 23

Directions: Find the words associated with Serena's life and career.

```
J G O L D M E D A L S Z O O M G W J
P I O C I A S L K K K U U Z N U Y E
Y O R K S H I R E T E R R I E R F H
H X D T L I D A C I A M A J J O U O
F L F L M A L S D N A R G L X D U V
Z W S Q E K T S I N N E T O Y K U A
Z C P L X G V P S R S E Q T U O P H
V R X O I F E C H R F T W O H V X S
D K X P H V I L S Y X Z L C V Q D W
V X K G N P B O X X K E O Q F O R I
P L V F M V K G V P G E M D C L P T
J Z B Y M I Y V T N M A T E Y A S N
P C L Z P N Y I A B D M A V X B H E
S O Y S A M H A W D R N H S K C M S
G M V D X P Y B X B S U U M N F G S
Q O O U L A E Y A 8 R C Z E B E P E
F V O S M X Y B F I S V R Q K L F S
G P D N Q A Z Z E N Y F F L O I Q S
```

Find These Words

TENNIS
OLYMPICS
JEHOVAHSWITNESSES
YORKSHIRETERRIER

GRANDSLAM
GOLDMEDALS
FRENCH

OCEANS8
MAYAANGELOU
JAMAICA

Directions: The images and text form a place Serena likes. Write the **sentence** below or the right number sequence.

#1

#2

#5 favorite

#3

#4 is

Directions: Read and answer the questions below. These are the different forms of poetry. There are clues in the puzzle to help you. Try and solve the cryptic message.

Clue for cryptic message: Serena's.

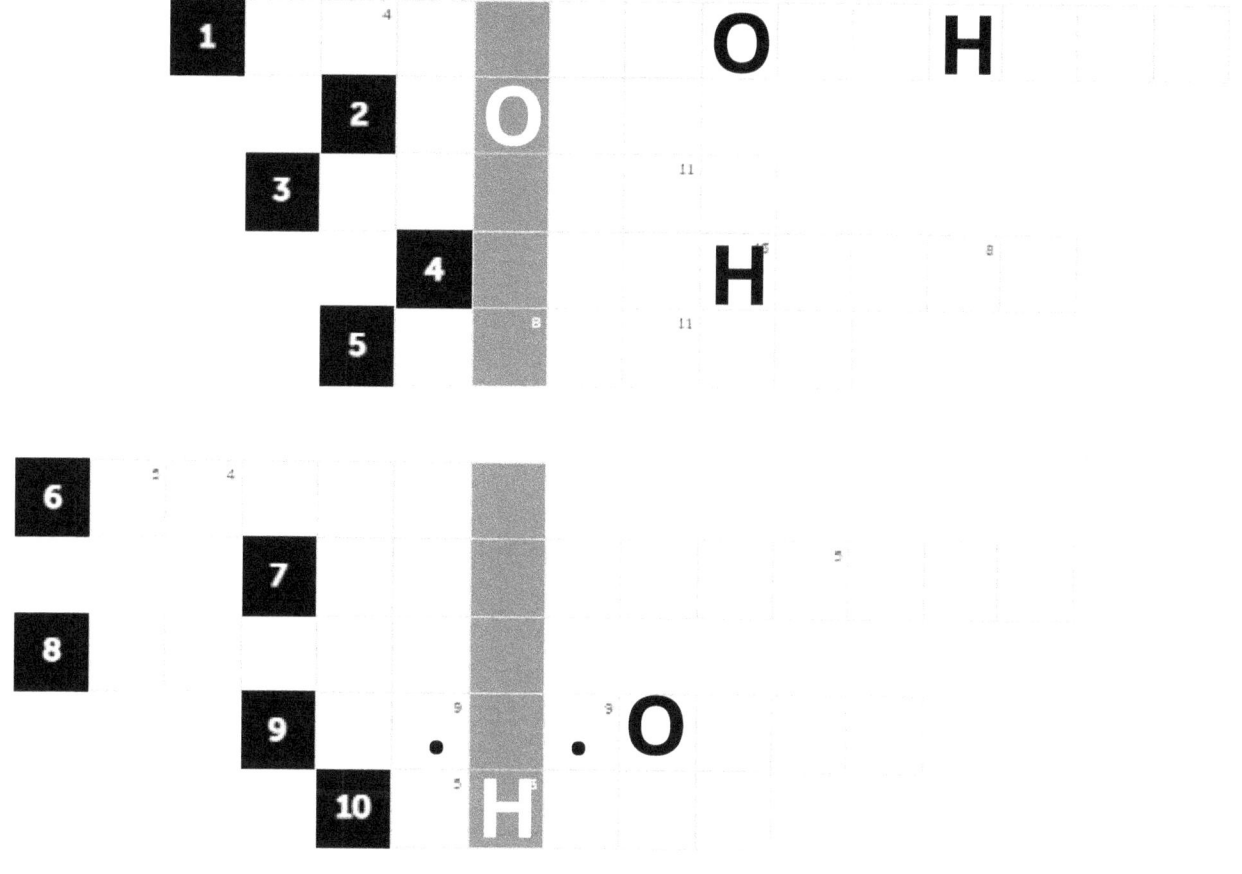

Questions

1) Serena is a minority shareholder in the _____.
2) Serena has won _____ gold medals in the Olympics.
3) Serena's middle name is _____.
4) Serena was born in Saginaw, _____.
5) Serena was _____ No 1 for 186 consecutive weeks.
6) Other than dogs, Serena favorite animals are _____.
7) Serena loves to watch _____ when she's not watching tennis.
8) Serena helped build a school in _____.
9) Serena won her first major title in 1999 at the _____.
10) Serena has competed at _____ Olympics.

Directions: This is the WGLT Challenge. Solve the cryptogram. As the puzzle solver, you need to find which number belongs to which character. And this can be pretty challenging! You will need to match the number with the letter. There are some letters given to you below. This will help you solve the other words and unlock more characters. **Good Luck.**

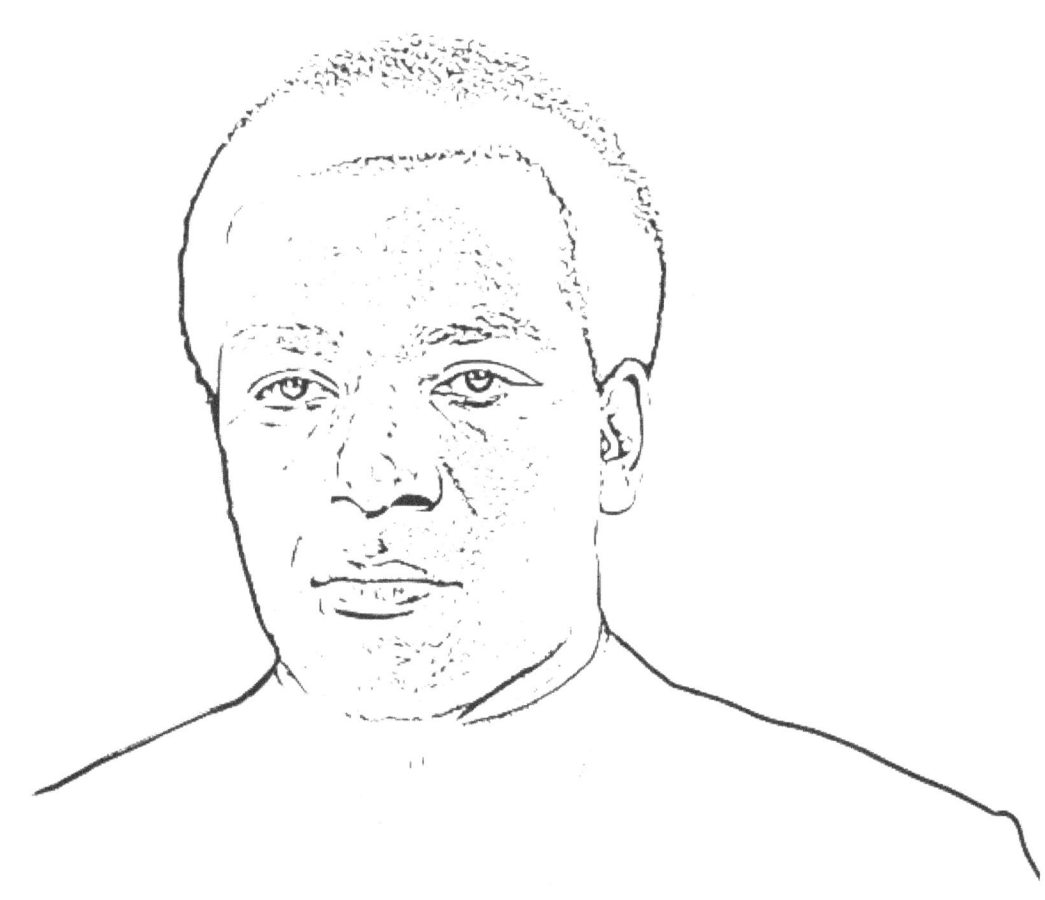

February 17, 1936 – Present
FOOTBALL PLAYER

99

James Brown

James Brown

James Brown

James Brown

James Brown

James Brown

Directions: read the bio below and answer the following questions.

Hi, my name is James Nathaniel Brown. I was born on February 17, 1936, in St. Simons Island, GA. I went to Manhasset High School in NY. I participated in football, lacrosse, baseball, basketball and track and field. I went to Syracuse University, where I also played football, basketball, track and lacrosse. I excelled in all of them, especially lacrosse. I'm in the Lacrosse Hall of Fame. While in college, I participated in the Reserve Officers' Training Corps. After graduating, I was commissioned as a second lieutenant in the Army. I served for four years as a captain. After I left the Army, I was drafted in the first round by the Cleveland Browns. After nine years in the NFL, I left as the NFL's record holder for both single-season touchdowns (1,863 in 1963) and career rushing touchdowns (12,312 yards), as well as the all-time leader in rushing touchdowns (106), total touchdowns (126) and all-purpose yards (15,549). I was the first player to reach the 100-rushing-touchdowns milestone. I'm the only rusher in NFL history to average over 100 yards per game for a career.

1. What college did I go to?
    A. Syracuse University
    B. Georgia University
    C. New York Central College
2. What rank was I when I left the Army?
    A. Major
    B. Captain
    C. Lieutenant
3. In my career I averaged _____ yards per game?
    A. 150
    B. 120
    C. 100

Directions: Answer the questions, to solve the crossword puzzle. You can use the internet if you get stuck on any question.

Across

1) Jim won one _____ with the Cleveland Browns.

2) Jim was also a great actor his first film was _____.

4) Jim was the lead actor in his film _____.

6) Jim led the NFL in each major rushing category (carries, yards, touchdown) ____ times.

7) Jim won MVP _____ times in his career.

Down

1) Jim is the only rusher in NFL history to average over 100 yards per game for a _____.

3) Jim went to _____ University where he played football, lacrosse and basketball.

5) Jim rushed for 1,000 yards in _____ of his nine seasons.

Directions: The images and text form an accomplishment of Jim Brown. Write the **sentence** below or the right number sequence.

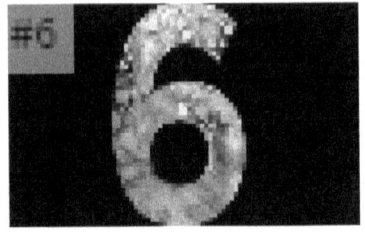
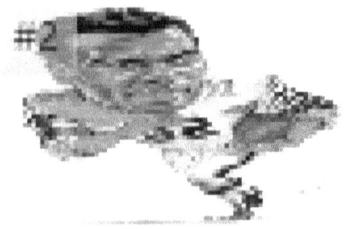

#7 The

104

Directions: Unscramble the words below about James. See if you can get the bonus word.

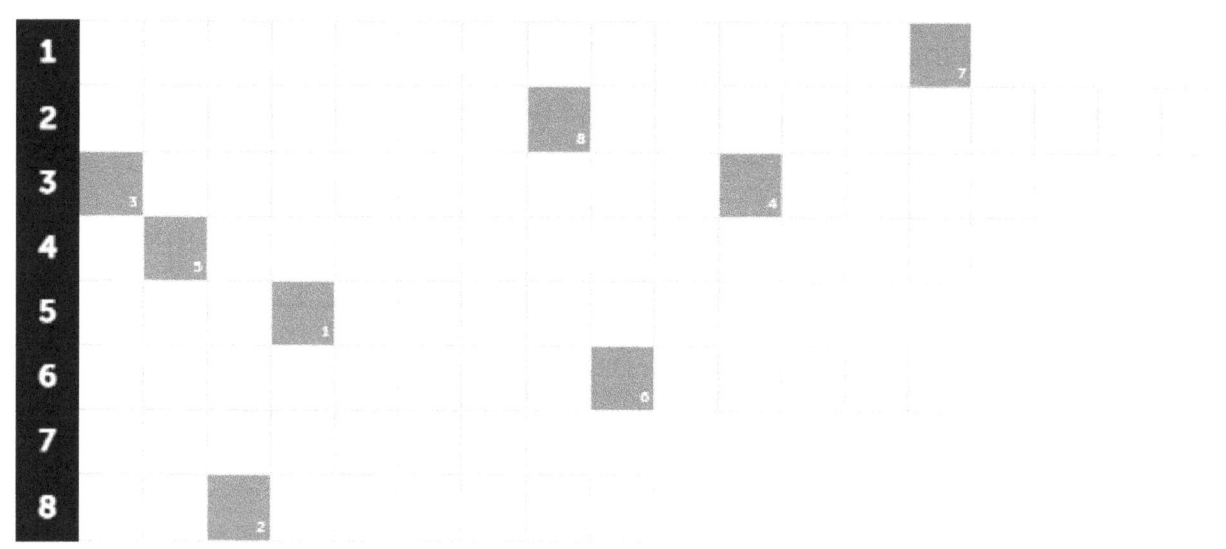

BONUS WORD

| 1 | 2 | 3 | 4 | 5 | 6 | 7 | 8 |

Unscramble Words

1) irznleykroswad
3) onadllwenrvsebc
5) amhfalfloe
7) rpboolw

2) scinyruturissvaeey
4) tkheaoiefrryooe
6) aedyynsuninagv
8) ognemenar

Directions: This is the WGLT Challenge. Solve the cryptogram. As the puzzle solver, you need to find which number belongs to which character. And this can be pretty challenging! You will need to match the number with the letter. There are some letters given to you below. This will help you solve the other words and unlock more characters. **Good Luck.**

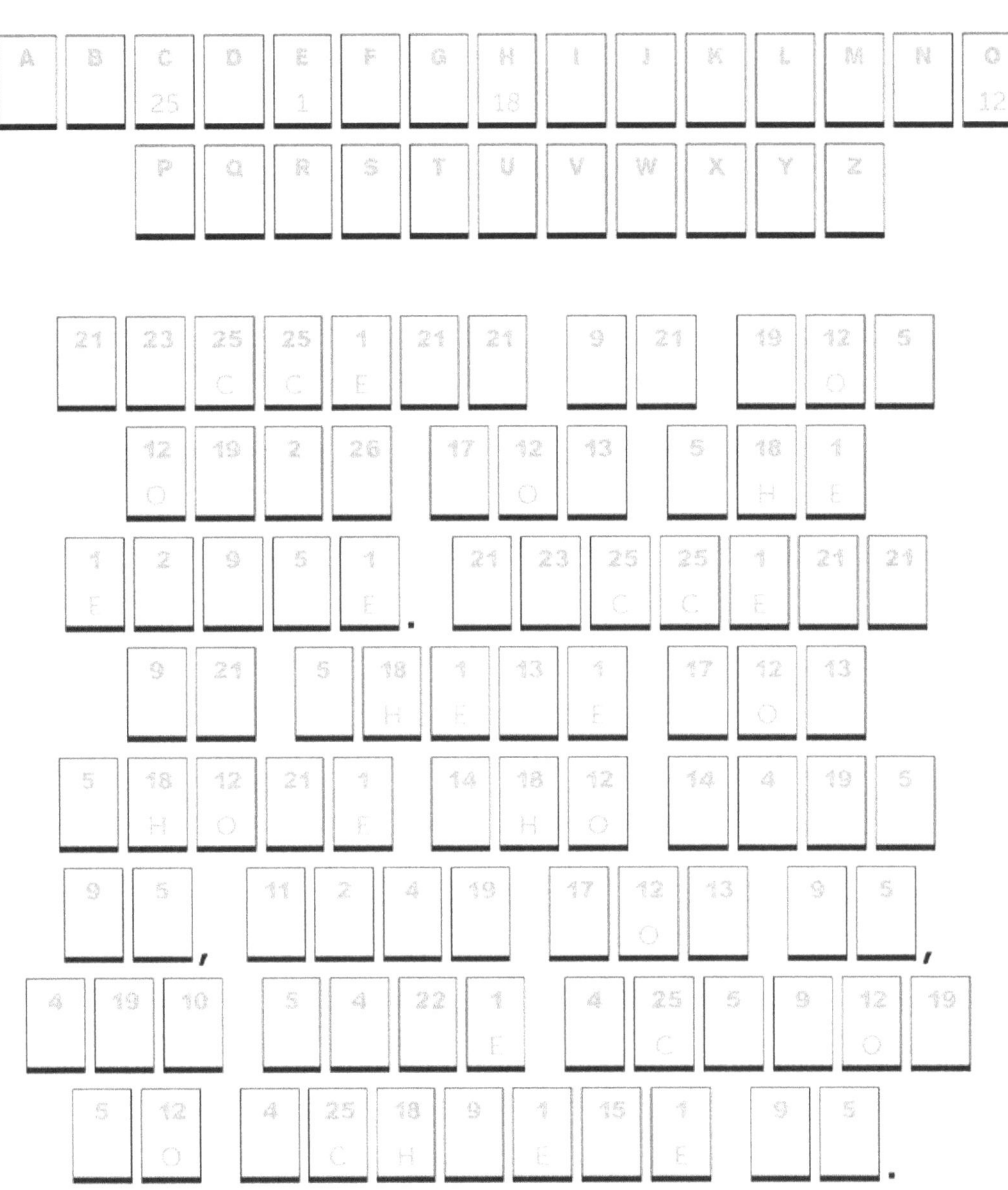

106

Henry Aaron

Henry Aaron

February 5, 1934 – January 22, 2021
BASEBALL PLAYER

LEFT BLANK ON PURPOSE

Henry Aaron

Henry Aaron

Henry Aaron

Henry Aaron

Henry Aaron

Henry Aaron

Directions: read the bio below and answer the following questions.

Hi, my name is Henry Aaron. I was born on February 5, 1934, in Mobile, AL. I attended Central High School, but they didn't have organized baseball, so I played outfield and third base for the Mobile Black Bears, which was a semipro team. I was also a member of the Boy Scouts of America. I signed my first contract with the Indianapolis Clowns of the Negro American League. After three months with the Indianapolis Clowns, I received two offers from MLB teams: The New York Giants and Boston Braves. The Braves offered $50 more a month, so I joined them. I played in the minors for three years and made my major league debut on April 15, 1954. Seven days later, I hit my first home run. I earned the nickname "Hammer" or "Hammerin' Hank" because of my long ball. I had 755 career home runs and broke the long-standing MLB record that had been set by Babe Ruth and stood as the most for 33 years.

1. What semipro team did I play for?
    A. Mobile Black Bears
    B. Chattanooga Lookouts
    C. Atlanta Crackers
2. What year did I make my MLB debut?
    A. 1951
    B. 1955
    C. 1954
3. What city was I born in?
    A. Birmingham
    B. Huntsville
    C. Mobile

Directions: Find the words associated with Hank's life and career.

```
U I H W A R S N U R E M O H 5 5 7 F W M
A D N I V E G U K O S Z K J W D M M S A
R T E D D E R O K F Z W L E M V I Q I J
O V Z V I I Y P U B U F C D N L R A G O
Q B W Y K A S L Z S O A L Q W U I L I R
A X L A V B N S M O D O G A E N G M C L
F A U S H U C P K I Y W U Z L M H G F E
D H T N W G U C O E Y K X K F Z T S M A
G N L L G N N K U L E E W I J A F S M G
H U V W A X M J N E I Y J H F O I Y V U
D K P A Y N W F B W Q S R T P S E P V E
N C N O C P T R Z P C C N N V L K B B
X Q H B O C E A R V F H S L P A D T F A
X V Z X E W D N B W M A P G O K E L B S
B W Z P E T U V H R R H H V G W R R O E
F H K R J M T I T L A P U T C J N O X B
A C S U I G P A H C H V F L H D S S R A
H M O S T V A L U A B L E P L A Y E R L
O C I L F X O Y Q L C K S S M C F C N L
N E G R O A M E R I C A N L E A G U E N
```

Find These Words

RIGHTFIELDER
ATLANTABRAVES
MILWAUKEEBREWERS
NEGROAMERICANLEAGUE

MAJORLEAGUEBASEBALL
755HOMERUNS
INDIANPOLISCLOWNS
MOSTVALUABLEPLAYER

Directions: The images and text form an accomplishment of Hank. Write the **sentence** below or the right number sequence.

#1  PLAYERS

#2 is

#7 Consider

#8  100

#3  Greatest

#4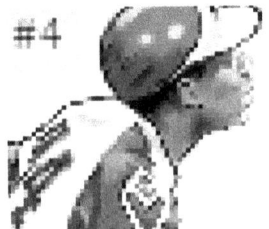

#6

#5 as

112

Directions: Read and answer the questions below. There are clues in the puzzle to help you. Try and solve the cryptic message.

Clue for cryptic message: Hank's nickname.

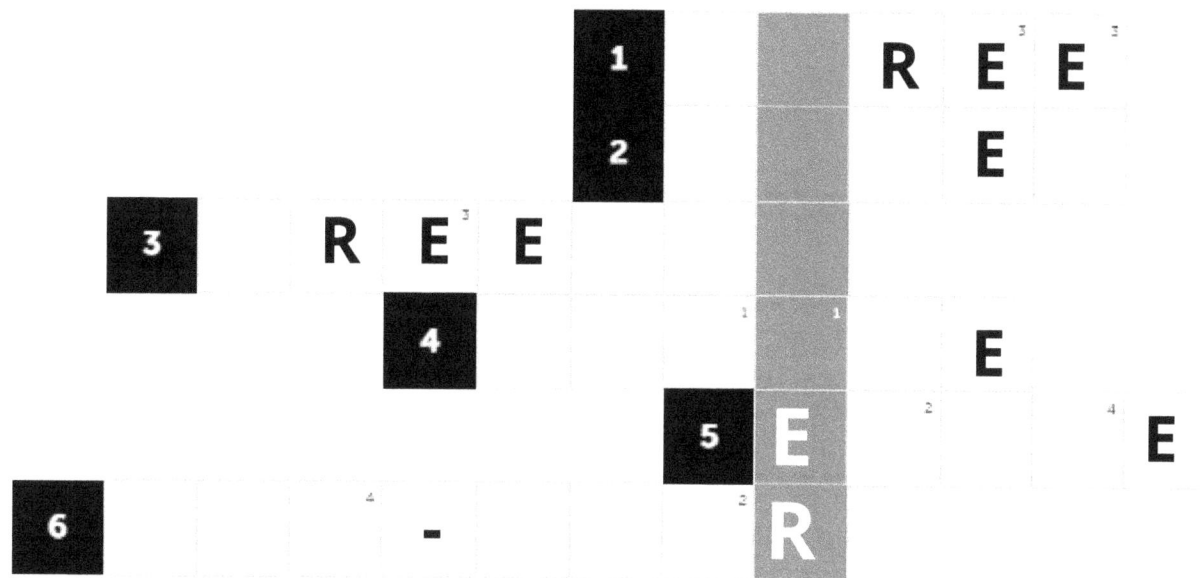

Questions

1) Has won ____ Gold Glove awards.
2) Hank is the all-time leader in total _____.
3) Hank was awarded the Presidential Medal of _____ by President Bush.
4) Hank played alongside his brother, _____, for seven seasons.
5) Hank was an ___ Scout.
6) Hank holds the record for most _____ Game appearances.

Directions: This is the WGLT Challenge. Solve the cryptogram. As the puzzle solver, you need to find which number belongs to which character. And this can be pretty challenging! You will need to match the number with the letter. There are some letters given to you below. This will help you solve the other words and unlock more characters. **Good Luck.**

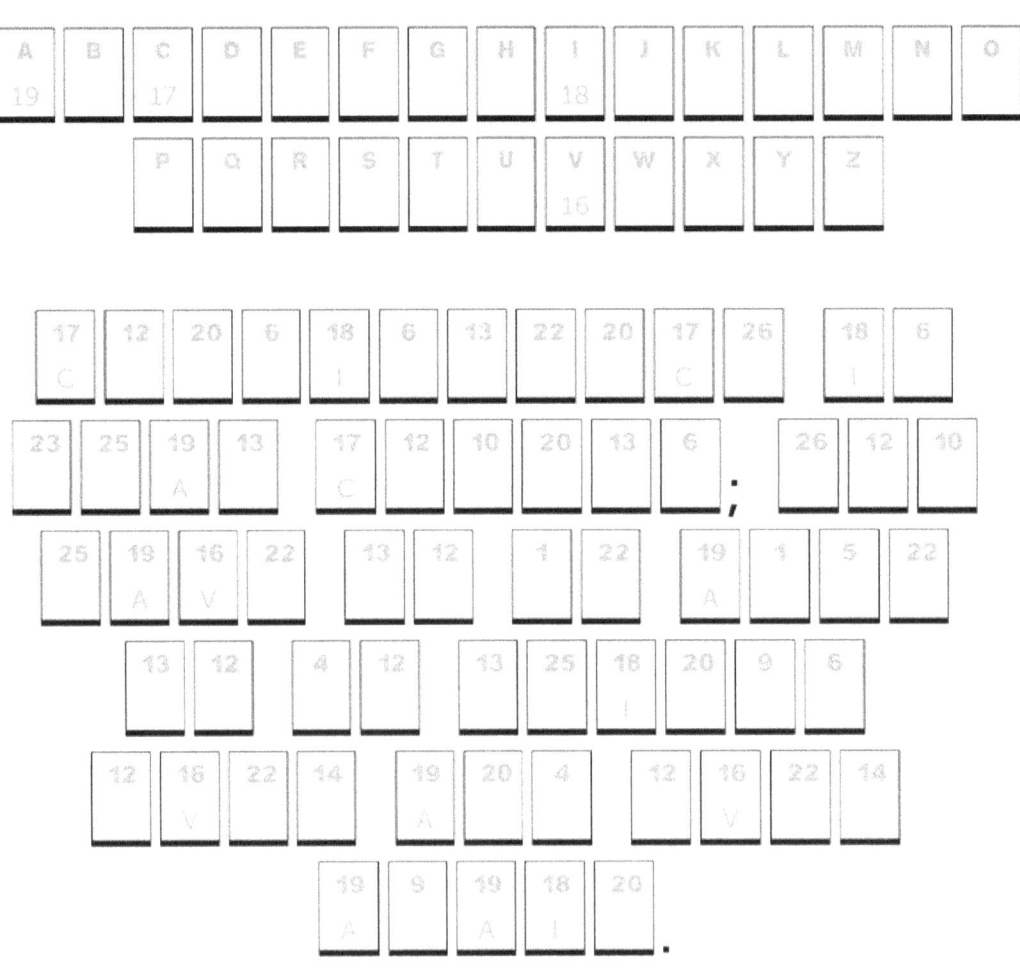

114

February 17, 1963 – Present
BASKETBALL PLAYER

LEFT BLANK ON PURPOSE

Michael Jordan

Michael Jordan

Michael Jordan

Michael Jordan

Michael Jordan

Michael Jordan

Directions: read the bio below and answer the following questions.

Hi, my name is Michael Jeffrey Jordan. I was born on February 17, 1963, in Fort Greene, Brooklyn, NY. I attended Emsley A. Laney High School and played basketball. I averaged around 25 points per game and was invited to play in the 1981 McDonald's All-American Game, where I scored 30 points. I went to the University of North Carolina. I made the game-winning jump shot in the 1982 NCAA Championship game against Georgetown. I went on to average 17.7 PPG on 54.0% shooting and added 5.0 RPG and 1.8 APG before being drafted by the Chicago Bulls in 1984. I signed with Nike that same year and started my signature shoe line, the Nike Air Jordans. I have won six NBA championships, six NBA Finals MVPs, five NBA MVPs and fourteen NBA All-Star games. In 1988, I was the first NBA player to win both the Defensive Player of the Year and Most Valuable Player awards in my career. Some consider me to be the Greatest of All Time (GOAT) in basketball. I'm the controlling owner of the NBA's Charlotte Hornets.

1. What NBA team drafted me?
    A. Washington Wizards
    B. Portland Trailblazers
    C. Chicago Bulls
2. How many NBA Championships have I won?
    A. 6
    B. 9
    C. 4
3. What shoe line did I start the Jordan brand under?
    A. Reebok
    B. Nike
    C. Puma

Directions: Answer the questions, to solve the crossword puzzle. You can use the internet if you get stuck on any question.

Across

1) Michael is the majority owner of the _____ Hornets.
5) Michael was named the NCAA College Player of the Year _____.
8) Michael went to the University of _____.
9) Michael loves to play ____ in his spare time.

Down

2) Michael was inducted into the _____ in 2009.
3) Michael won ten _____ titles during his career.
4) Michael wore number twenty-three, twelve and _____ during his career.
6) Michael starred in the original _____ movie.
7) Michael's dad inspired him to play _____.

Directions: The images and text form an accomplishment of Michael's. Write the **sentence** below or the right number sequence.

#6 3

#7 2

#9 won

#1 CHAMPIONSHIPS

#5 (NBA logo)

#8 (Michael Jordan)

#4 6

#3 (three trophies)

#2 and

8, 4, 2, 7, 5, 1, 9, 6, 3

Directions: Unscramble the words below about Michael. See if you can get the bonus word.

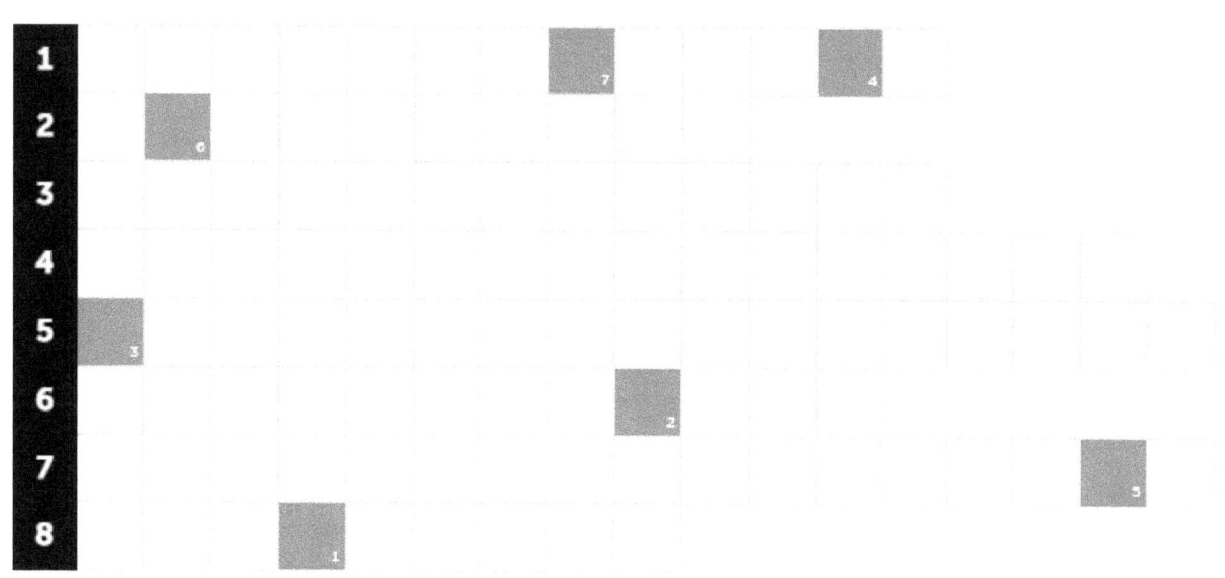

BONUS WORD

Unscramble Words

1) iohicpsnhmasp
2) kbaltbalse
3) nhrtaocorilna
4) rtrteeoahcstolhn
5) orayalmbputvsllee
6) coacslgbulih
7) ltteteelofasrmiga
8) aiordanjr

121

Directions: This is the WGLT Challenge. Solve the cryptogram. As the puzzle solver, you need to find which number belongs to which character. And this can be pretty challenging! You will need to match the number with the letter. There are some letters given to you below. This will help you solve the other words and unlock more characters. **Good Luck.**

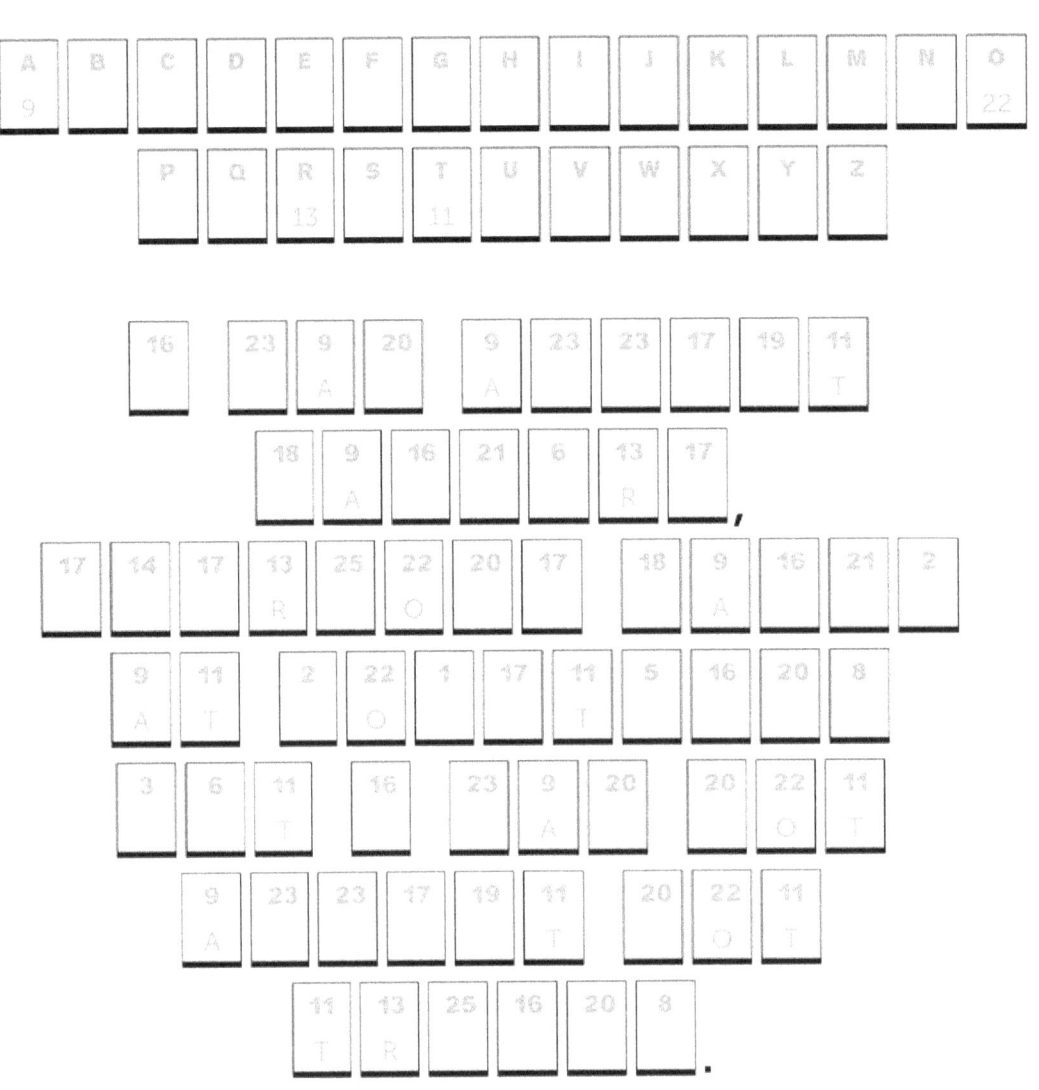

122

123

June 23, 1940 – November 12, 1994
TRACK AND FIELD

Wilma Rudolph

Wilma Rudolph

Wilma Rudolph

Wilma Rudolph

Wilma Rudolph

Wilma Rudolph

Directions: read the bio below and answer the following questions.

Hi, my name is Wilma Rudolph. I was born on June 23, 1940, in Saint Bethlehem, TN. I attended Burt High School, where I excelled in basketball and track. After having my first child, I enrolled at Tennessee State University (TSU). I became a part of the Delta Sigma Theta sorority while at TSU and graduated with a bachelor's degree in education. At 15, I qualified to compete in the 200-meter individual event at the 1956 Summer Olympics in Melbourne, Australia. I also ran the third leg of the 4x100-meter relay. My team and I took home the bronze medal after matching the world record time of 44.9 seconds. In 1960 at the Summer Olympics in Rome, Italy, I competed in three events: the 100- and 200-meter sprints, as well as the 4×100-meter relay. I won a gold medal in each of these events and became the first American woman to win three gold medals in a single Olympiad. I set the world record for all three events: 11.2 seconds in the 100-meter sprint, 22.9 seconds in the 200-meter sprint and 44.4 seconds in the 4x100-meter relay.

1. What college did I go to?
   A. Texas University
   B. Tennessee University
   C. Temple University
2. What Olympics did I win 3 gold medals?
   A. 1956 Summer Olympics
   B. 1964 Summer Olympics
   C. 1960 Summer Olympics
3. How old was I when I won my first Olympic medal?
   A. 19
   B. 17
   C. 15

Directions: Find the words associated with Wilma's life and career.

```
X I U O I A R F C V Z 2 O Z N B F V
X G M N O I T K N D F O J Z T G W W
A M O Z L J P V Y M B O X K E Y R O
L Q R L A B C S Q X N M K B N V X I
N K L A D L J J F G L E A Q N A F A
S A Z P E M P B F S A T M K E G O I
W P C D M G E H A W I E T K S Q H X
H O R I E C B D L D I R H K S C X N
J W K I Z Q X I A A K D E K E A N B
U R W A N E Z Q N L A A T X E I T Q
L H U G O T K M A A S S O S S Q H W
U E N H R U E P N M Z H R P T P E M
M X W O B T W R R O V N N A A E F N
H E D L E I F D N A K C A R T G L W
T L J B S O K T E E D H Y E D A J
Q S L C Z H C F L F T N O H H A S O
A T C F Y U X I S C I P M Y L O H N
N U H S A D R E T E M 0 0 1 X K C C
```

Find These Words

TRACKANDFIELD   GOLDMEDALS   OLYMPICS
200METERDASH   SPRINTER   THETORNADO
THEFLASH   BRONZEMEDAL   100METERDASH
TENNESSEESTATE

Directions: The images and text form an accomplishment of Wilma's. Write the **sentence** below or the right number sequence.

#8 an

#1

#5

#6 in

#7

#4 ICON

#3 INTERNATIONAL

#2 was

Directions: Read and answer the questions below. These are the different forms of poetry. There are clues in the puzzle to help you. Try and solve the cryptic message.

Clue for cryptic message: Wilma's nickname.

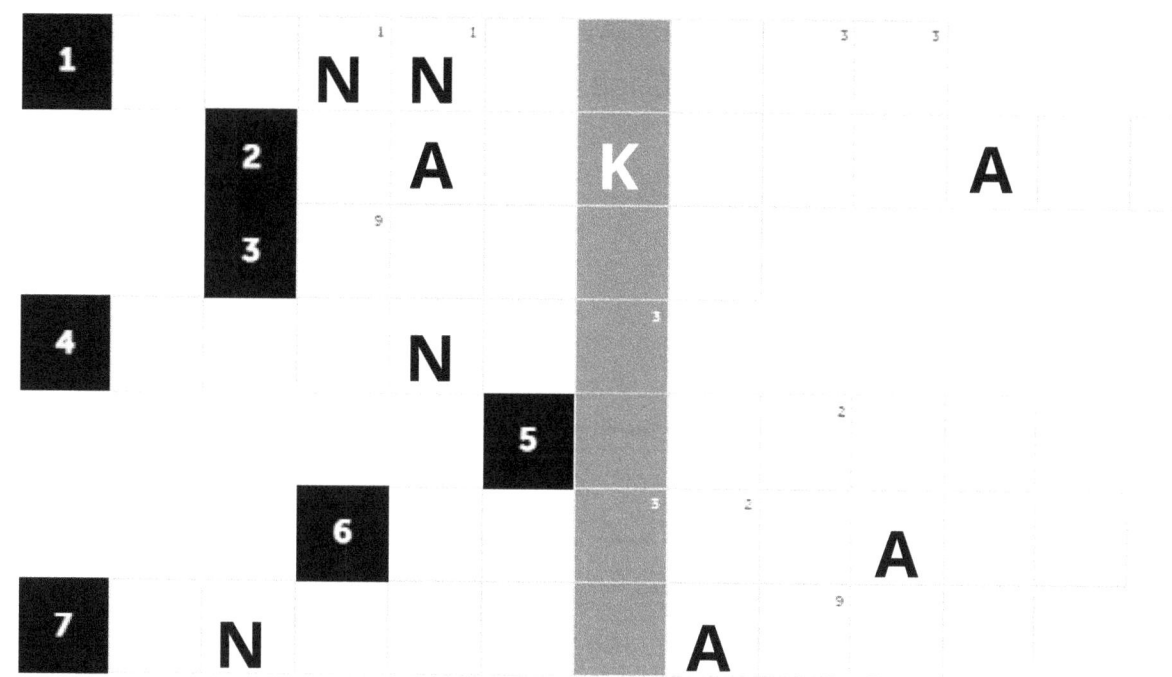

Questions

1) Wilma graduated from _____ State University with a bachelor's degree in education.

2) Wilma played _____ at Clarksville's Burt High School.

3) Wilma was the first woman in America to win _____ gold medals in the same Olympics.

4) Wilma was sixteen when she won her first _____ medal at the Olympics.

5) Wilma held _____ world records when she retired.

6) Wilma _____ polio as a child.

7) Wilma's homecoming parade and banquet were the first fully _____ municipal events in her hometown Clarksville.

129

Directions: This is the WGLT Challenge. Solve the cryptogram. As the puzzle solver, you need to find which number belongs to which character. And this can be pretty challenging! You will need to match the number with the letter. There are some letters given to you below. This will help you solve the other words and unlock more characters. **Good Luck.**

Usain St. Leo Bolt

Usain St. Leo Bolt

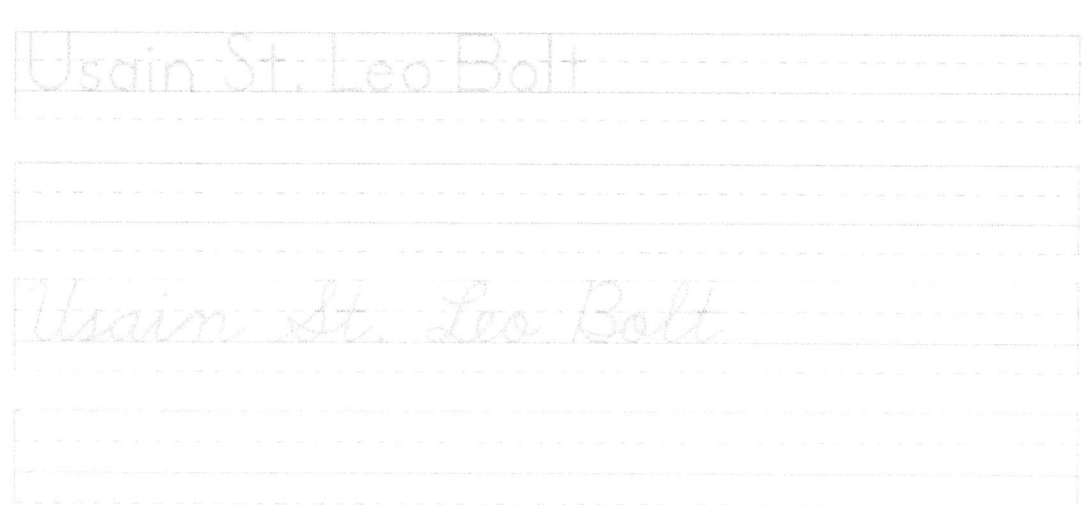

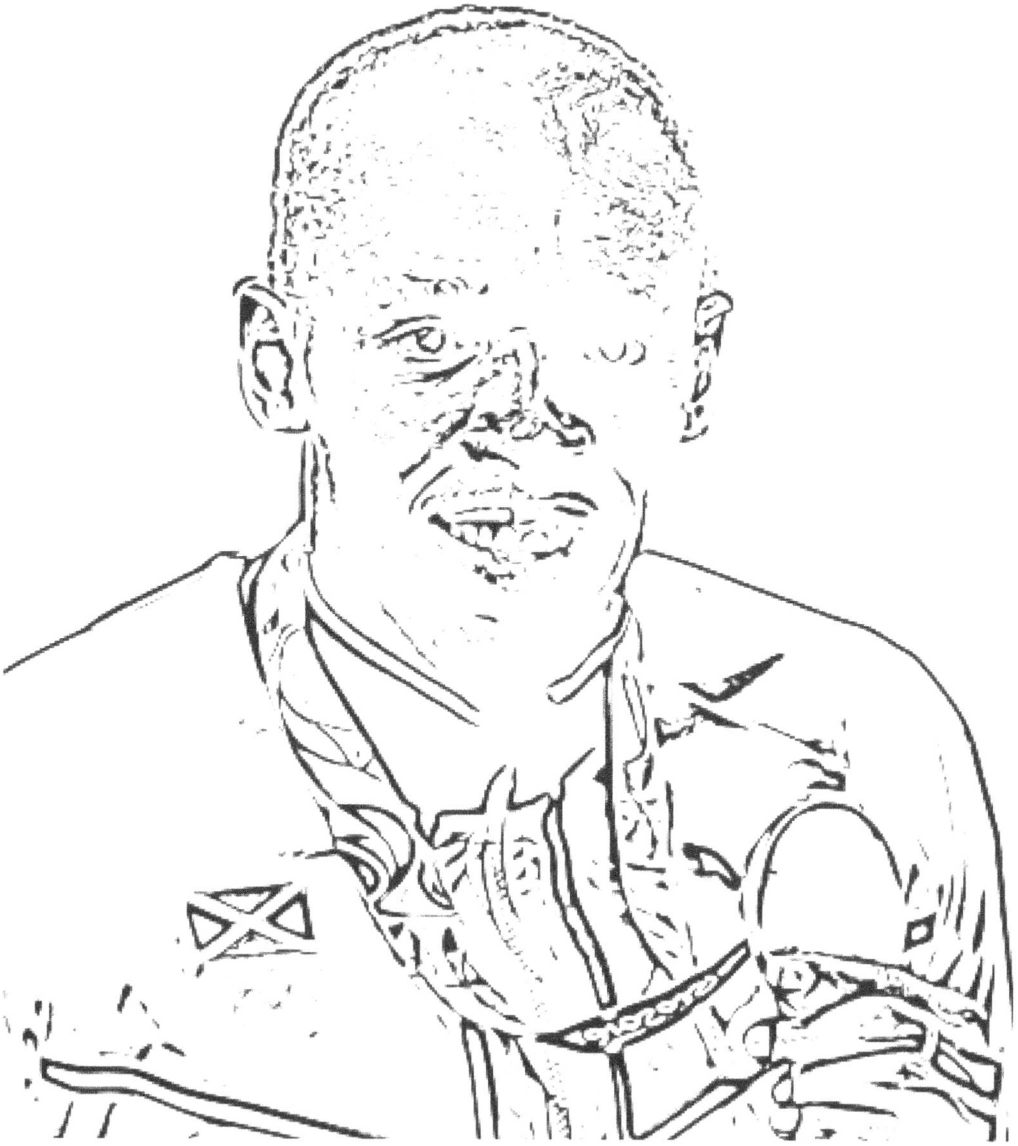

August 21, 1986 – Present
TRACK AND FIELD

LEFT BLANK ON PURPOSE

Usain St. Leo Bolt

Usain St. Leo Bolt

Usain St. Leo Bolt

Usain St. Leo Bolt

Usain St. Leo Bolt

Usain St. Leo Bolt

Directions: read the bio below and answer the following questions.

Hi, my name is Usain St. Leo Bolt. I was born on August 21, 1986, in Sherwood Content, which is a small town in Jamaica. I attended William Knibb Memorial High School and played cricket and ran track and field. I won my first high school championship medal in 2001. I won the silver medal in the 200-meter event with a time of 22.04 seconds. I am one of only nine athletes to win world championships at the youth, junior and senior levels of an athletic event. As of 2022, I'm the world record holder in the 100-meter sprint, 200-meter sprint and 4×100-meter relay. I'm also the only sprinter to win Olympic 100-meter and 200-meter titles at three consecutive Olympics (2008, 2012 and 2016). I have won a total of twenty-three gold medals, five silver medals and one bronze medal in my career. My achievements as a sprinter have earned me the media nickname "Lightning Bolt."

1. When did I win my first medal?
    A. College
    B. Olympics
    C. High School
2. What year did I first win Olympic gold in 100 and 200 m?
    A. 2004
    B. 2008
    C. 2012
3. What is my nickname from the media?
    A. Black Lightning
    B. Flash
    C. Lightning Bolt

Directions: Answer the questions, to solve the crossword puzzle. You can use the internet if you get stuck on any question.

Across

1) Usain is the first athlete to win six gold medals in ____.
4) The media gave Usain the nickname "Bolt from the ____".
6) Usain is the first man to achieve the '_____' by winning both 100m and 200m games in 2008 and 2012 Olympics consecutively.
7) Usain is one of only ____ athletes to win World Championships at the Youth, Junior and Senior level.

Down

1) Usain suffers from ____.
2) Usain holds the world record in the ____ with 9.58 seconds.
3) Usain holds the world record in the ____ with 19.19 seconds.
5) Usain has a clothing line on his named ____ Bolt Collection.

Directions: The images and text form an accomplishment of Usain. Write the **sentence** below or the right number sequence.

#1

CHOICE

#6

#2

first

#5

#4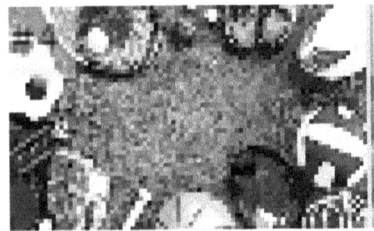

#3

was

136

Directions: Unscramble the words below about Usain. See if you can get the bonus word.

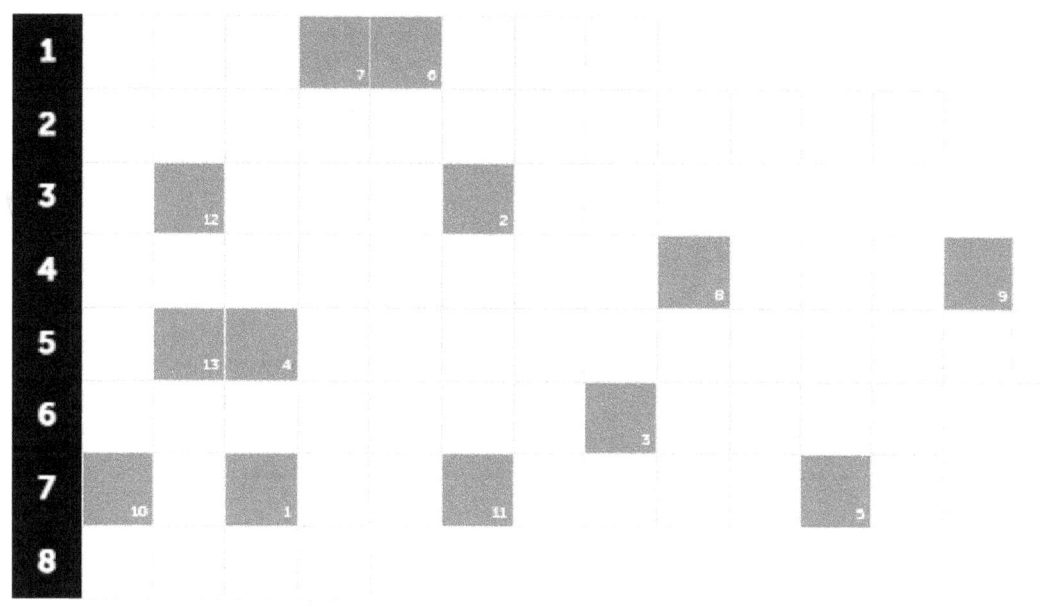

BONUS WORD

1 2 3 4 5 6 7 8 9 10 11 12 13

Unscramble Words

1) nrpteisr **2)** rosdrdrleowc **3)** smyicolp
4) ocvhnoyeatvlgi **5)** eyearltathtfeohe **6)** amaacgriefts
7) mltiyitbbolo **8)** ampu

Directions: This is the WGLT Challenge. Solve the cryptogram. As the puzzle solver, you need to find which number belongs to which character. And this can be pretty challenging! You will need to match the number with the letter. There are some letters given to you below. This will help you solve the other words and unlock more characters. **Good Luck.**

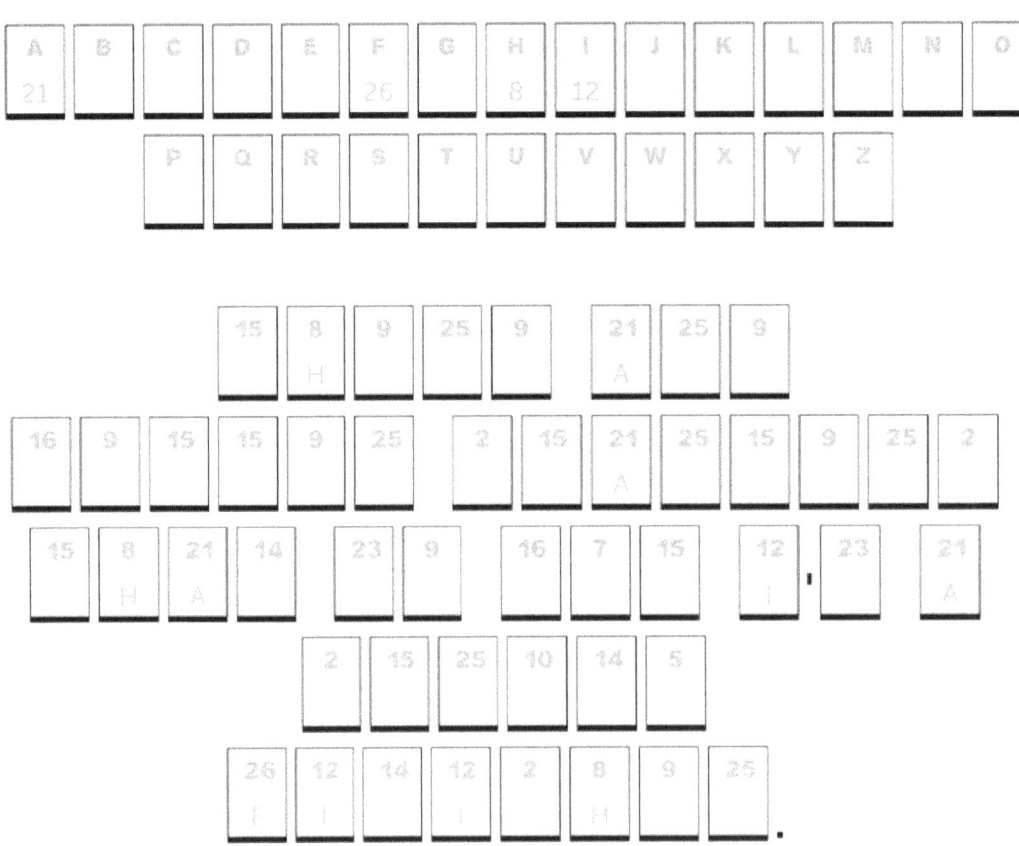

Earl Lloyd

Earl Lloyd

139

April 3, 1928 – February 26, 2015
BASKETBALL PLAYER

Earl Lloyd

Earl Lloyd

Earl Lloyd

Earl Lloyd

Earl Lloyd

Earl Lloyd

Directions: read the bio below and answer the following questions.

Hi, my name is Earl Lloyd. I was born on April 3, 1928, in Alexandria, VA. I attended Parker-Grey High School. I received a scholarship to play basketball at West Virginia State University (WVSU). In school, my nickname was "Moon Fixer" because of my size and my skill as a defensive specialist. My team and I won two Central Intercollegiate Athletic Association (CIAA) Conference and Tournament Championships in 1948 and 1949. I graduated from WVSU with a bachelor's degree in physical education in 1950. I was drafted by the Washington Capitals in the 1950 NBA draft and gained a new nickname: "The Big Cat." I was the first African American to play a game in the NBA and scored six points on October 31, 1950, which was Halloween night. In 1954 and 1955, I averaged career highs of 10.2 points and 7.7 rebounds for the Syracuse Nationals. We beat the Fort Wayne Pistons four games to three to win the 1955 NBA Championship. Jim Tucker and I became the first African Americans to play on an NBA championship team.

1. What year did I win the NBA Championship?
    A. 1955
    B. 1949
    C. 1960
2. What college did I go to?
    A. Indian University
    B. Virginia University
    C. West Virginia State University
3. What is not my nickname?
    A. The Big Cat
    B. Moon Fixer
    C. The D-Man

Directions: Find the words associated with Earl's life and career.

```
Q M P L V O H E A D C O A C H H B N
Y J X A Z I K E M A F F O L L A H T
O W Z L D W L Q S C A X W E F W Z I
W A S H I N G T O N C A P I T O L S
F V Y K B M I R S P O U G G X H Z F
N L Q J P A K W T Z S K W J Q W I V
S Y R A C U S E N A T I O N A L S S
G U C U K X W K I T X X L P W C Y N
O P O G P Y I O E L K M J Y U Y B P
U N I T E D S T A T E S A R M Y Y G
Z C K U K K Q S N A B I R E G V P S
U B C O L L E G E C H A M P I O N H
E O I Y X S U O G B B V L D N T Z A
L L G N H T S K L W Z X K L Q U A Q
K R D B T I N B A C H A M P I O N B
P H Y S I C A L E D U C A T I O N H
P F A S S I S T A N T C O A C H U H
N L S N G T E G J Z B X S O L E B L
```

Find These Words

BASKETBALL
SYRACUSENATIONALS
UNITEDSTATESARMY
HALLOFFAME
COLLEGECHAMPION

ASSISTANTCOACH
WASHINGTONCAPITOLS
HEADCOACH
NBACHAMPION
PHYSICALEDUCATION

Directions: The images and text form an accomplishment of Earl's. Write the **sentence** below or the right number sequence.

#1  Korean

#2 the   #6 in

#5

#4  WAR   #3

Directions: Read and answer the questions below. These are the different forms of poetry. There are clues in the puzzle to help you. Try and solve the cryptic message.

Clue for cryptic message: This is Earl's nickname.

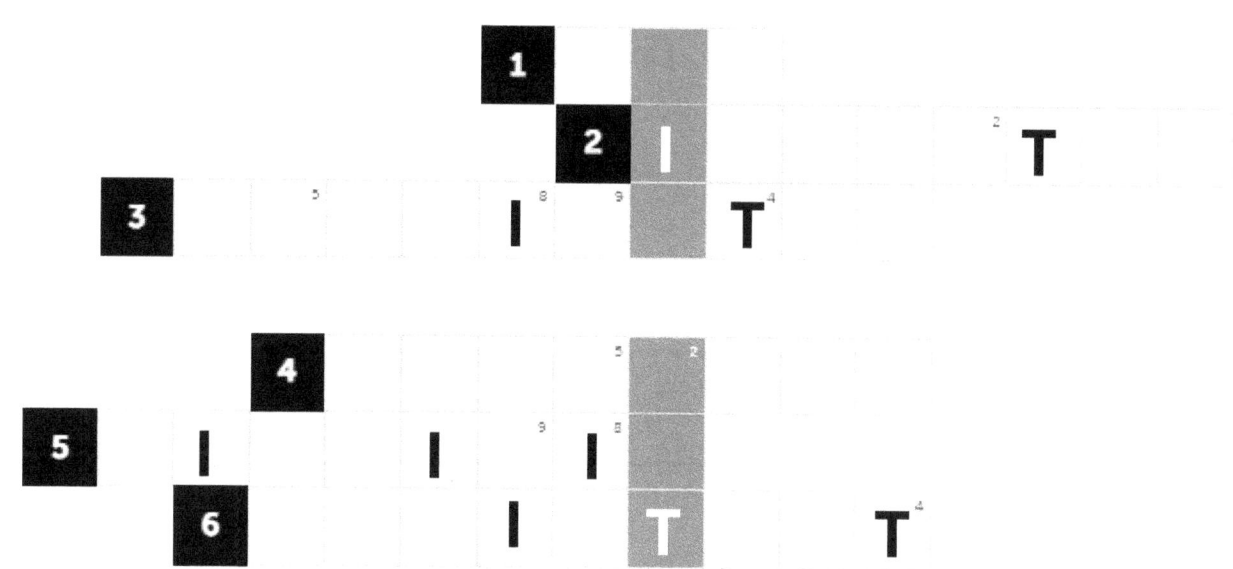

Questions

1) Earl was the first African American player to play a game in the _____.

2) Earl was _____ into the Naismith Basketball Hall of Fame.

3) Earl was drafted in the nineth round with pick #100 by the _____ Capitols in the 1950 NBA draft.

4) Earl helped lead the _____ Nationals to the 1955 NBA Championship.

5) Earl led West _____ State to two Central Intercollegiate Athletic Association Conference and Tournament Championships.

6) Earl was the first African-American _____ coach.

Directions: This is the WGLT Challenge. Solve the cryptogram. As the puzzle solver, you need to find which number belongs to which character. And this can be pretty challenging! You will need to match the number with the letter. There are some letters given to you below. This will help you solve the other words and unlock more characters. **Good Luck.**

146

Anthony Dungy

Anthony Dungy

October 6, 1955 - Present
FOOTBALL COACH/PLAYER

Anthony Dungy

Anthony Dungy

Anthony Dungy

Anthony Dungy

Anthony Dungy

Anthony Dungy

Directions: read the bio below and answer the following questions.

Hi, my name is Anthony Dungy. I was born on October 6, 1955, in Jackson, MI. I attended Parkside High School. I played college football at the University of Minnesota and was the Gophers' most valuable player as a quarterback in 1975 and 1976. I wasn't drafted by the NFL, but I signed with the Pittsburgh Steelers as a free agent and was converted to defensive back. My best season was in 1978, which is when I intercepted six passes and we won Super Bowl XIII. I went into coaching after that. I'm the first NFL head coach to defeat all 32 NFL teams. I was also the youngest assistant coach at 25 and the youngest coordinator at 28 in NFL history. I was also the first African American coach to win a Super Bowl, which was Super Bowl XLI.

1. What position did I play in college football?
    A. Quarterback
    B. Running Back
    C. Defensive Back
2. How many Super Bowls did I win?
    A. 1
    B. 3
    C. 2
3. How old was I when I became an assistant coach ?
    A. 28
    B. 24
    C. 25

Directions: Answer the questions, to solve the crossword puzzle. You can use the internet if you get stuck on any question.

Across
4) Tony won the Super Bowl XLI with the _____ Colts.
6) Tony was the _____ assistant coach in NFL history, at twenty-five.
7) Tony was the first African-American coach to win a _____ in the NFL.
8) Tony won Super Bowl XIII with the _____ Steelers

Down
1) Tony was the head coach of the _____ Bay Bucs.
2) Tony was the _____ person to win a title as a player and as a head coach.
3) Tony is a sports _____ on NBC's Football Night in America.
5) Tony is the first NFL head coach to _____ all thirty-two NFL teams.

Directions: The images and text form an accomplishment of Tony. Write the **sentence** below or the right number sequence.

Directions: Unscramble the words below about Anthony. See if you can get the bonus word.

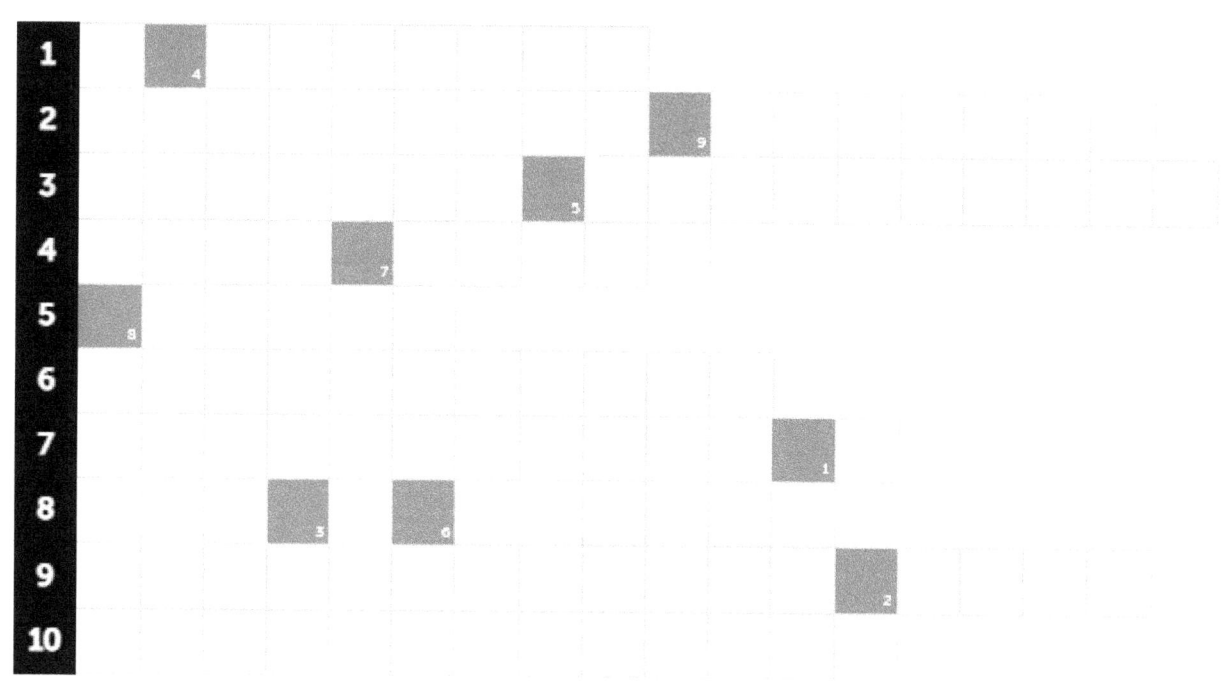

BONUS WORD

Unscramble Words

1) eaachchod
2) oindatnaislcoilps
3) estbserguettphslir
4) hpghoetser
5) nnigniw
6) tuacbrakrqe
7) tstsarnaplosy
8) tpusbmaaaycb
9) iclsnruscdotepien
10) ncebseaeivdkf

153

Directions: This is the WGLT Challenge. Solve the cryptogram. As the puzzle solver, you need to find which number belongs to which character. And this can be pretty challenging! You will need to match the number with the letter. There are some letters given to you below. This will help you solve the other words and unlock more characters. **Good Luck.**

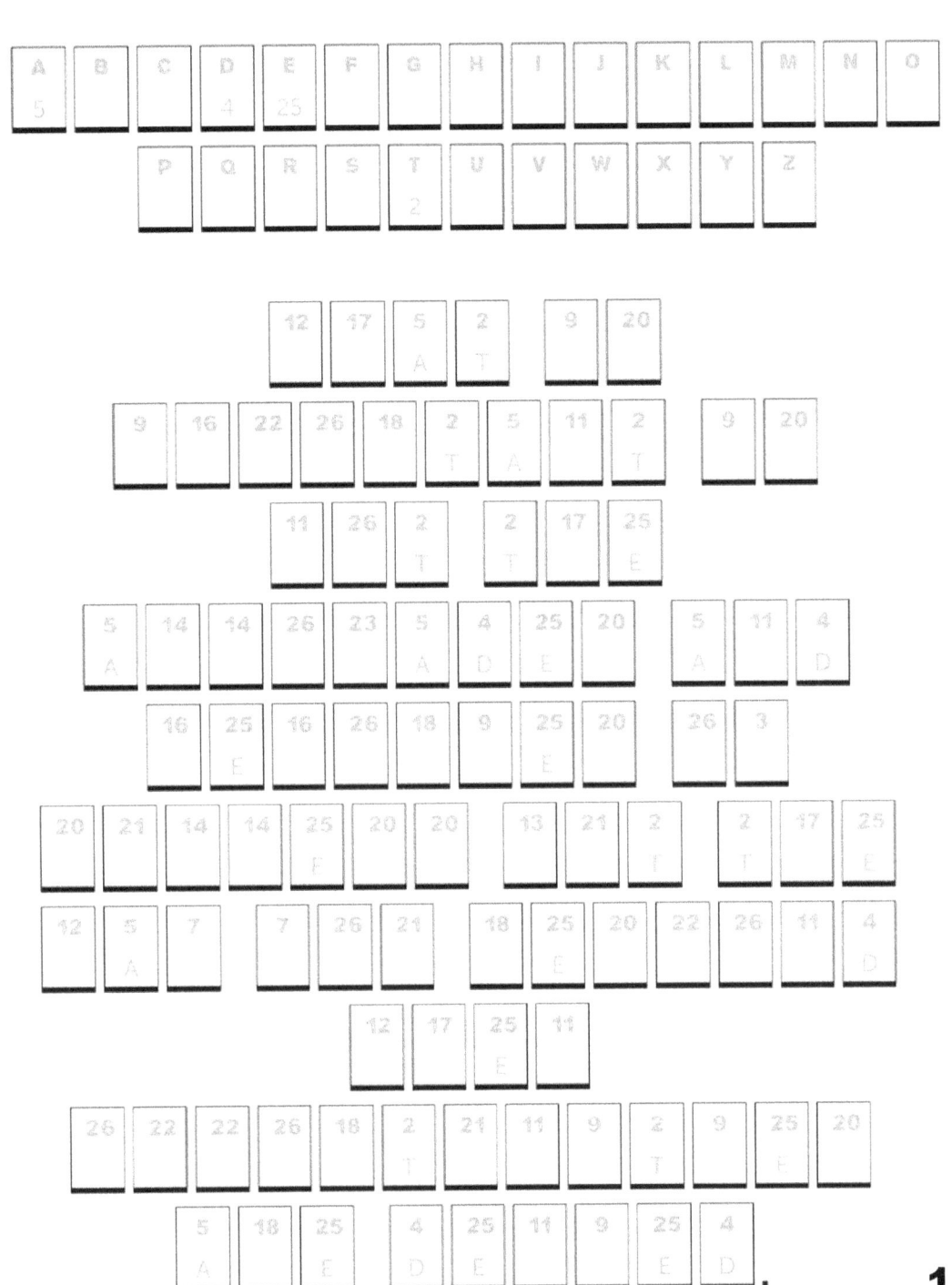

154

Candace Parker

Candace Parker

April 19, 1986 - Present
BASKETBALL PLAYER

155

LEFT BLANK ON PURPOSE

Candace Parker

Candace Parker

Candace Parker

Candace Parker

Candace Parker

Candace Parker

Directions: read the bio below and answer the following questions.

Hi, my name is Candace Parker. I was born on April 19, 1986, in St. Louis, MO. I attended Naperville Central High School. I was 15 years old when I made my first dunk as a sophomore. I led my high school basketball team to Class AA state titles in 2003 and 2004 and compiled a school record of 2,768 points (22.9 points per game) and 1,592 rebounds (13.2 rebounds per game). I'm the only two-time award winner of the USA Today High School Player of the Year Award. I won the award in 2003 and 2004. I announced my commitment to Tennessee on ESPNEWS, which made me the first women's player to announce an oral commitment live on the network. While at Tennessee, my team and I won two consecutive national championships (2007 and 2008). I was the first woman to dunk in an NCAA tournament game and the first woman to dunk twice in a college game. I won two WNBA championships, one WNBA Finals MVP, two WNBA MVPs and six WNBA All-Star appearances.

1. How old was I when I first dunked?
    A. 15
    B. 18
    C. Never
2. How many WNBA championships have I won?
    A. None
    B. 3
    C. 2
3. What college did I go to?
    A. University of Connecticut
    B. Notre Dame
    C. Tennessee

Directions: Find the words associated with Candace's life and career.

```
M X L N Y Z W X P D B T C B S N U T
V O A P H A D I D A S V A J Z M A N
W G S H X Z H I O X N S O C C E R L
N N W T B D M Q J W K G T G S V Z L
F J B R V Z N Q Y E X L H L E L R A
A T Y A E A W O T L F K O B P G D B
I Y V J C B L B I K A V G R L N Z Y
W R H A K H A U W P E A J Z R L J E
H J P W B L A O B E M G G Y H U C L
H J T Z L U G M S L K A K C N V M L
P I D P M Q W S P S E V H U O E A O
U X H J L B E B G I C P H C Q E P V
U S N B Y N M J O B O I L E A T D N
Z G F N N E T B X K C N P A B A M D
E D W E X C F E S W V D S M Y I C R
T Q T V O J G Q A P R D P M Y E D N
F I E E R C X U S L V C I B V L R Y
R K C T Q B D Z P M R E K N U D O I
```

Find These Words

ADIDAS
DUNKER
VOLLEYBALL
SOCCER
TENNESSEEVOLS
MOSTVALUBLEPLAYER
NCAACHAMPION
BASKETBALL
WNBACHAMPION
OLYMPICS

Directions: The images and text form an accomplishment of Candace's. Write the **sentence** below or the right number sequence.

 #1

#6

#5 the

#2 Played

#4 for

 #3

160

Directions: Read and answer the questions below. These are the different forms of poetry. There are clues in the puzzle to help you. Try and solve the cryptic message.

Clue for cryptic message: Candace's shoe.

Questions

1) Candace is part owner of the _____ City Football Club.
2) Candace is the first WNBA player to appear on the _____ of an NBA 2K game.
3) Candace was the first player to win _____ of the Year and Most Valuable Player (MVP) in the same season.
4) Candace won two _____ Most Valuable Player (MVP) awards.
5) Candace was the first woman to _____ in an NCAA tournament game.
6) Candace was a three-time Ms. Basketball of _____.
7) Candace has two _____ medals in the Olympics.
8) Candace was selected as the first overall pick in the 2008 WNBA Draft by the Los Angeles _____.
9) Candance is an NBA _____ on TNT.

161

Directions: This is the WGLT Challenge. Solve the cryptogram. As the puzzle solver, you need to find which number belongs to which character. And this can be pretty challenging! You will need to match the number with the letter. There are some letters given to you below. This will help you solve the other words and unlock more characters. **Good Luck.**

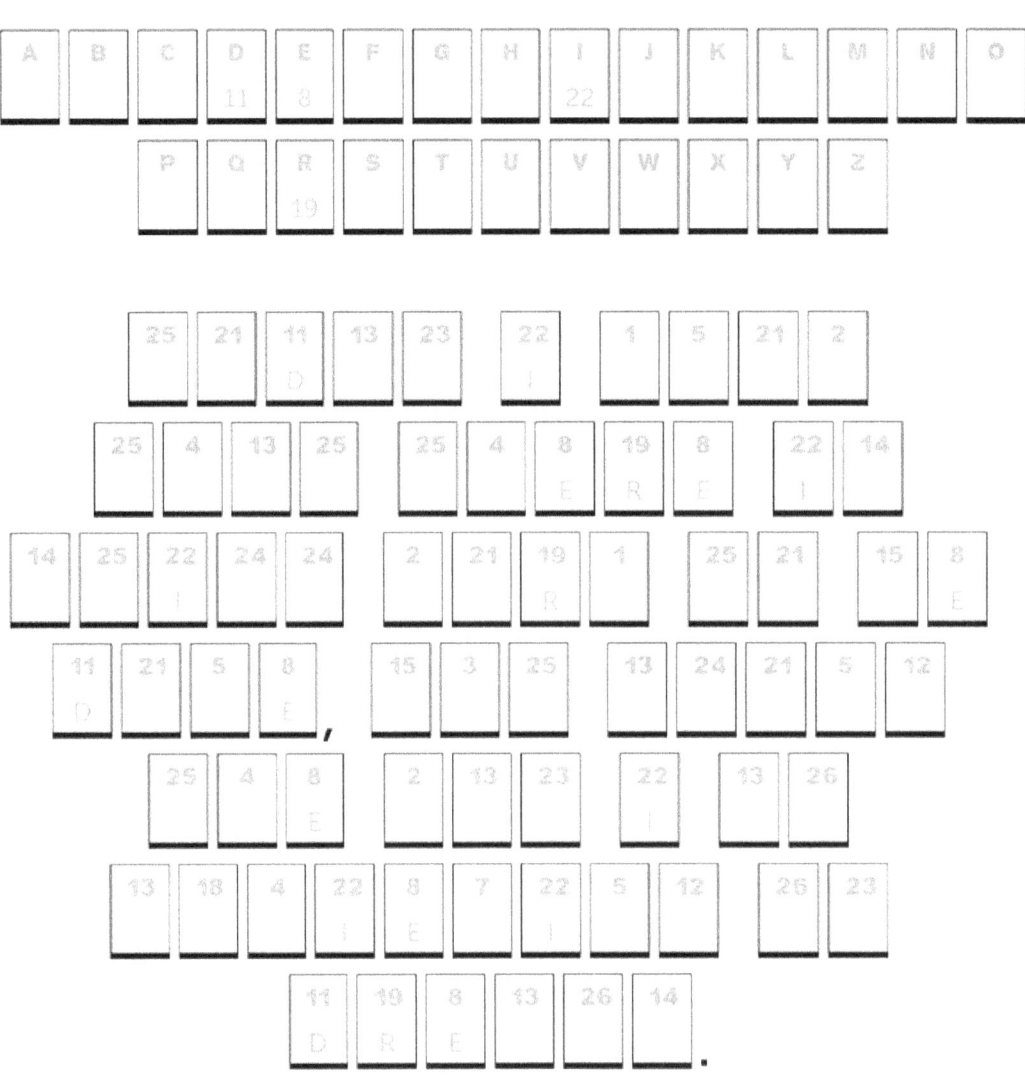

Shani Davis

Shani Davis

August 13, 1982 - Present
SPEED SKATER

Shani Davis

Shani Davis

Shani Davis

Shani Davis

Shani Davis

Shani Davis

Directions: read the bio below and answer the following questions.

Hi, my name is Shani Davis. I was born on August 13, 1982, in Chicago, IL. I attended Marquette Senior High School. I earned spots on both the long-track and short-track teams at the 1999 Junior World Championship and simultaneously made the national team. In 2000, I made history by becoming the first U.S. skater to make the long- and short-track teams at the Junior World Teams. I became the first African American skater to earn a spot on a short-track team. I made the 2002 Winter Olympics short-track team. I'm also the only U.S. skater to ever make both the short-track and the long-track Junior World teams three years in a row. At the 2006 Winter Olympics, I became the first African American athlete to win a gold medal in an individual event at the Olympic Winter Games by winning the 1000-meter speedskating event. I'm also the first man to win back-to-back 1000-meter Olympic speed skating gold medals.

1. What was the first year I made the Olympics team?
   A. 2006
   B. 2002
   C. 2004
2. I made what team 3 years in a row?
   A. Olympic Team
   B. World Team
   C. Junior World Team
3. What event did I win my gold medal in?
   A. 500 meter
   B. 1000 meter
   C. 1500 meter

Directions: Answer the questions, to solve the crossword puzzle. You can use the internet if you get stuck on any question.

Across

1) Shani is the first black athlete to win an individual gold medal at a _____ Games.
3) Shani has _____ gold medals in the Olympics.
5) Shani has won ten careers _____ World Cup titles.
6) Shani was the first man to _____ defend the 1000 meters.
8) Shani held world records in the _____ and 1,500-meter events.

Down

2) Shani set _____ world records in 2005.
4) Shani has set a total of nine _____ records.
7) Shani won a _____ medal in the 1500-meter event at the Olympic Winter Games

Directions: The images and text form something about Shani. Write the **sentence** below or the right number sequence.

#1

is #7  #3

#2

a #6

#4  #5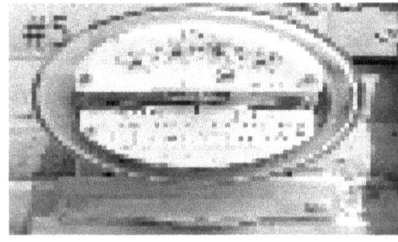

Directions: Unscramble the words below about Shani. See if you can get the bonus word.

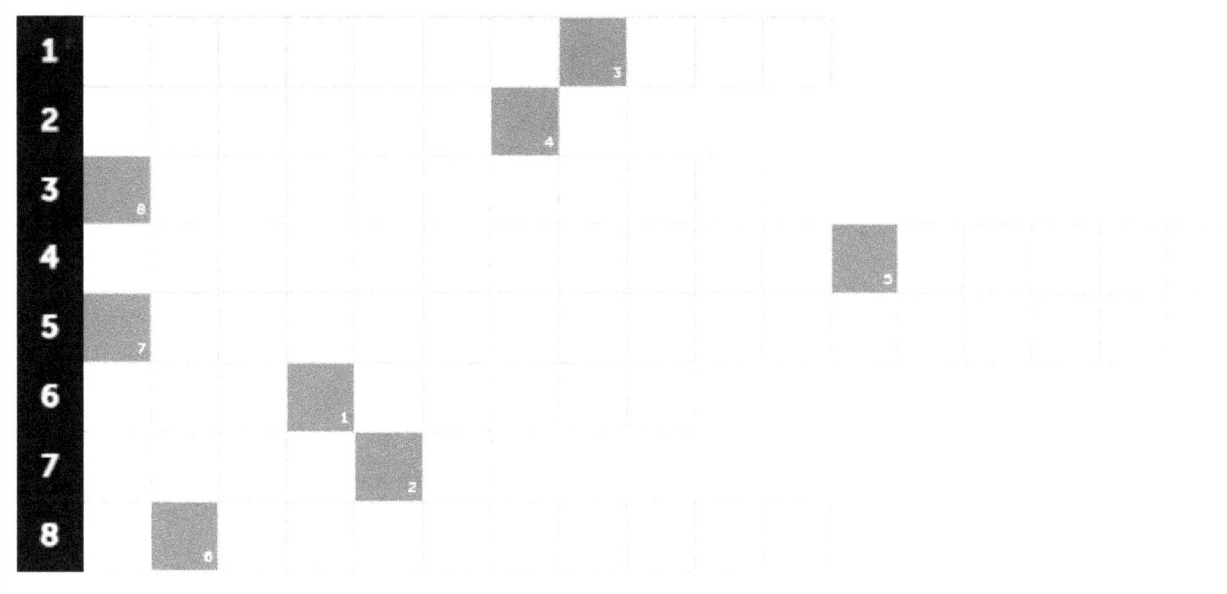

BONUS WORD

1 2 3 4 5 6 7 8

Unscramble Words

1) epksdseater   **2)** icyspmol   **3)** dsomlgelad
4) rerddecrorlwodolh   **5)** eoghrhmaicintnrn   **6)** avnvrcoeu
7) soowmc   **8)** amegtersiwn

Directions: This is the WGLT Challenge. Solve the cryptogram. As the puzzle solver, you need to find which number belongs to which character. And this can be pretty challenging! You will need to match the number with the letter. There are some letters given to you below. This will help you solve the other words and unlock more characters. **Good Luck.**

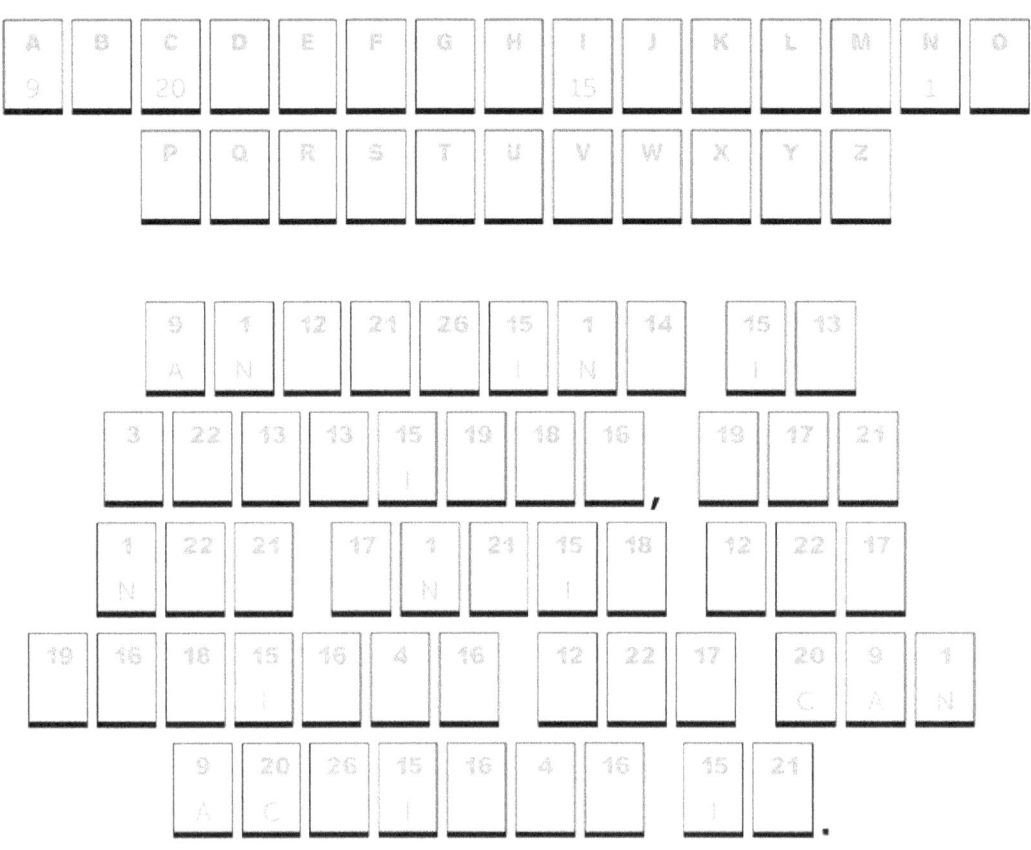

Simone Biles

Simone Biles

March 14, 1997 - Present
GYMNAST

Simone Biles

Simone Biles

Simone Biles

Simone Biles

Simone Biles

Simone Biles

Directions: read the bio below and answer the following questions.

Hi, my name is Simone Biles. I was born on March 14, 1997, in Columbus, OH. Unfortunately, my birth mother could not care for me, so my maternal grandfather adopted me and raised me in Spring, TX. I was homeschooled due to my training. I graduated in 2015. At age 24, I've already made history. Not only am I the first female gymnast to win three World All-Around titles in a row, but I'm also the first Black gymnast to become the World All-Around champion. I'm the most decorated female gymnast in the US. As of 2022 I've won 25 medals at the World Championships. Nineteen of them were gold. I'm the first U.S. citizen to win a medal in every event at this competition. I'm also the first woman ever to successfully land the Yurchenko double pike in a competition. I have four skills named after me. One is on the vault, one is on the balance beam and two are on the floor exercise.

1. **How many World Championship medals have I won?**
   A. 25
   B. 19
   C. 32
2. **I was the first black gymnast to win this championship?**
   A. Olympics
   B. Junior Championships
   C. World All-Around Championships
3. **I'm the first woman to successfully land what?**
   A. Double back flip
   B. Front double twist
   C. Yurchenko double pike

Directions: Find the words associated with Simone's life and career.

```
V B O O M C X A B J O Z X L Q P G Z
G E A E Q H L J I L F A U E E Y S L
O S F L V R W X Y C R I Y F M W E G
L D L O A D K M P K N J I N X O S O
D L O A K N P I L L G W A S C R F K
M R O V I I C D S A Q S K S D L X D
E U R P C Y L E C H T A Q Q H D D G
D N E S B K Q E B I C A C X P C M O
A E X G G I Y I C E E X G W U H B S
L Q E P W X L S R C A G E J N A O X
S G R G O W Z E N C E M D K I M P E
C J C W C X P K S F T I Q I S P U L
J K I O V P N H L T L F Y A H I U N
G M S T N B G J W R W B R I E O G T
M S E S F V W M L O E O N E X N J L
W F O Y U R C H E N K O D D S O C U
W M Z A I Q J X A W C T P E Z F V A
G R E A T E S T O F A L L T I M E V
```

Find These Words

BILESTWO   GYMNASTICS   GOLDMEDALS
OLYMPICS   FLOOREXERCISE   VAULT
WORLDCHAMPION   BALANCEBEAM   GREATESTOFALLTIME
YURCHENKO

Directions: The images and text about Simone. Write the **sentence** below or the right number sequence.

#5 MEETS

#8 after

#2 herself

#4 (pizza)

#1 TREATS

#3 (cookies)

#6 to

#7 (Simone)

176

Directions: Read and answer the questions below. There are clues in the puzzle to help you. Try and solve the cryptic message.

Clue for cryptic message: This is a move of Simone's.

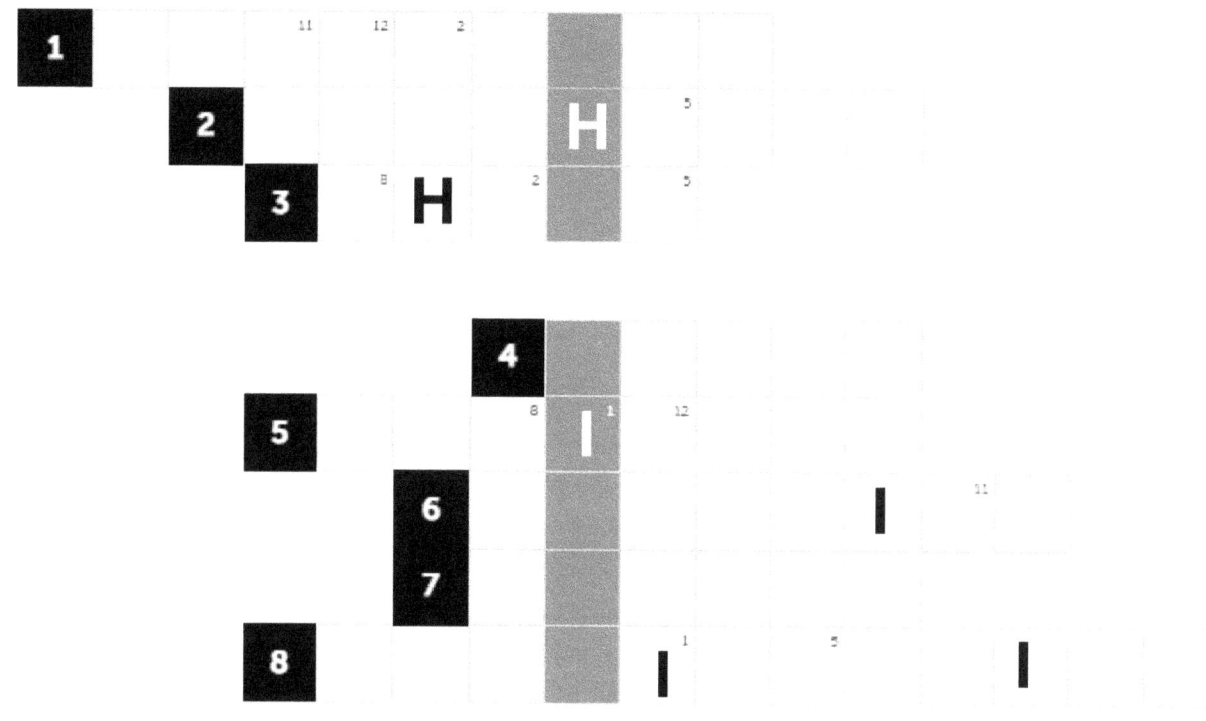

Questions

1) Simone is the most _____ female gymnast in America.

2) Simone is the first woman to complete a _____ double pike skill on vault.

3) Simone is the first female gymnast to win _____ world all-around titles in a row.

4) Simone is the first _____ gymnast to become the world all-around champion.

5) Simone won six _____ all-around titles.

6) Simone has won six gold medals in the _____.

7) Simone has a record twenty-five world championship _____.

8) Simone was awarded the _____ Medal of Freedom.

Directions: This is the WGLT Challenge. Solve the cryptogram. As the puzzle solver, you need to find which number belongs to which character. And this can be pretty challenging! You will need to match the number with the letter. There are some letters given to you below. This will help you solve the other words and unlock more characters. **Good Luck.**

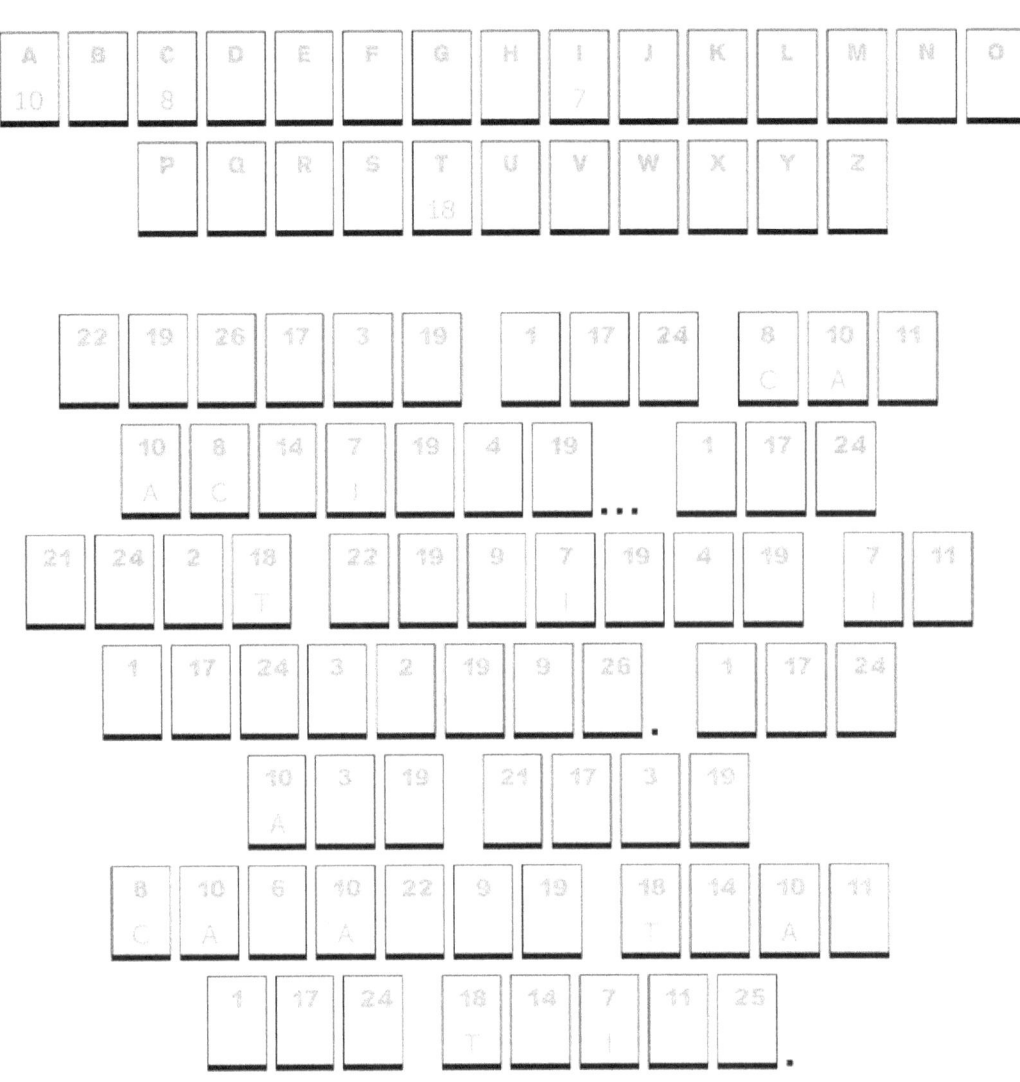

Cullen Jones

February 29, 1984 - Present
SWIMMER

Cullen Jones

Cullen Jones

Cullen Jones

Cullen Jones

Cullen Jones

Cullen Jones

Directions: read the bio below and answer the following questions.

Hi, my name is Cullen Jones. I was born on February 29, 1984, in the Bronx, NY. I attended Saint Benedict's Preparatory School in Newark, NY. While there, I set numerous Essex County swimming records. I attended North Carolina State University in 2003, where I studied English and swam for the swimming and diving teams. I became a professional swimmer in the summer of 2006 after I signed with Nike. Later that year, I set a meet record in the 50-meter freestyle with a time of 21.84 seconds. I also swam a leg (split of 47.96) in the world-record-breaking 4×100 meter freestyle relay, along with Michael Phelps, Neil Walker and Jason Lezak. During the 2008 Summer Olympics, I became the first African American to hold a world record in swimming (4×100 meter freestyle relay). As part of the American team, I hold the world record in the 4×100 meter freestyle relay.

1. What city was I born in?
    A. Manhattan
    B. New York City
    C. Bronx
2. What year did I sign with Nike?
    A. 2003
    B. 2006
    C. 2008
3. What event did I set a meet record in?
    A. 50 meter
    B. 100 meter
    C. 200 meter

Directions: Answer the questions, to solve the crossword puzzle. You can use the internet if you get stuck on any question.

Across

2) Cullen is the first African-American to hold a _____ (4×100-meter freestyle relay) in swimming.
4) Cullen won a ____ medal in 4×100-meter freestyle relay in the 2007 World Aquatics Championships.
5) Cullen was the first African-American man to win gold medal at the World _____ Games.
7) Cullen won ____ medal in the 50-meter freestyle.
8) Cullen best events are _____ sprint events.

Down

1) Cullen won three medals at the 2012 Summer ____.
3) Cullen holds the world record in the 4×100-meter freestyle _____ (long course).
6) Cullen help. children learn to swim with the Make a _____ foundation.

Directions: The images and text form an accomplishment of Charlie. Write the **sentence** below or the right number sequence.

#7 got

#6 BACHELOR'S

#2

#1 a

#3 in

#5 ENGLISH

#4

Directions: Unscramble the words below about Cullen. See if you can get the bonus word.

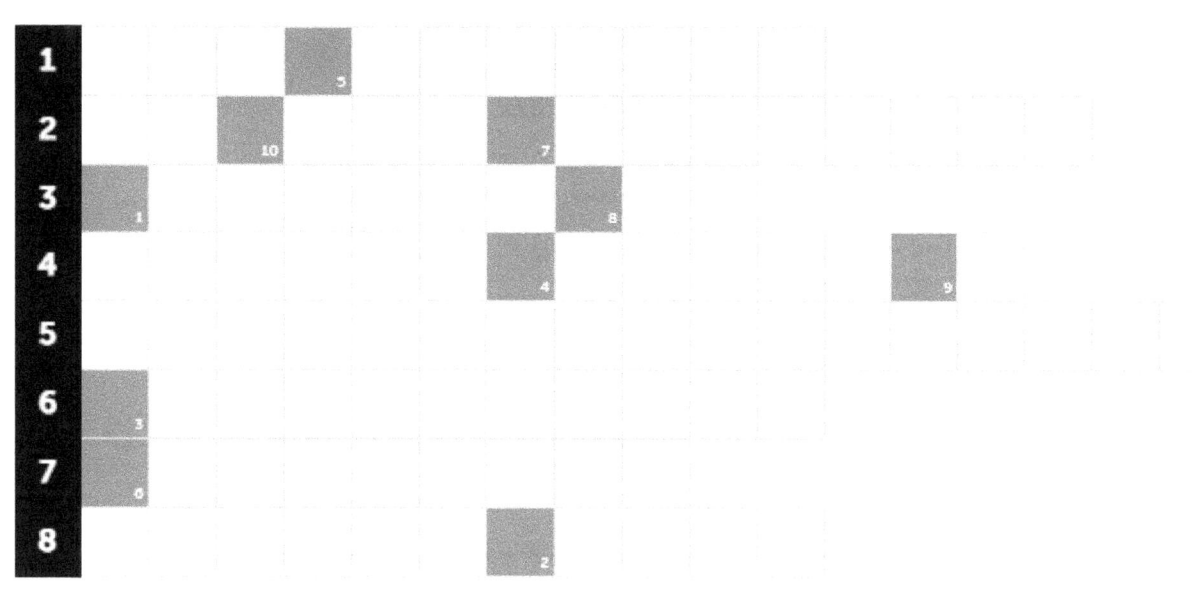

BONUS WORD

1　2　3　4　5　6　7　8　9　10

Unscramble Words

1) amleyeledry　　**2)** oeslptasauamhkr　　**3)** omddellsga
4) crmmypseoimlus　　**5)** CttrvisiyNeetaSUn　　**6)** cwodrrdorle
7) ytfeelser　　**8)** ytosencxuse

185

Directions: This is the WGLT Challenge. Solve the cryptogram. As the puzzle solver, you need to find which number belongs to which character. And this can be pretty challenging! You will need to match the number with the letter. There are some letters given to you below. This will help you solve the other words and unlock more characters. **Good Luck.**

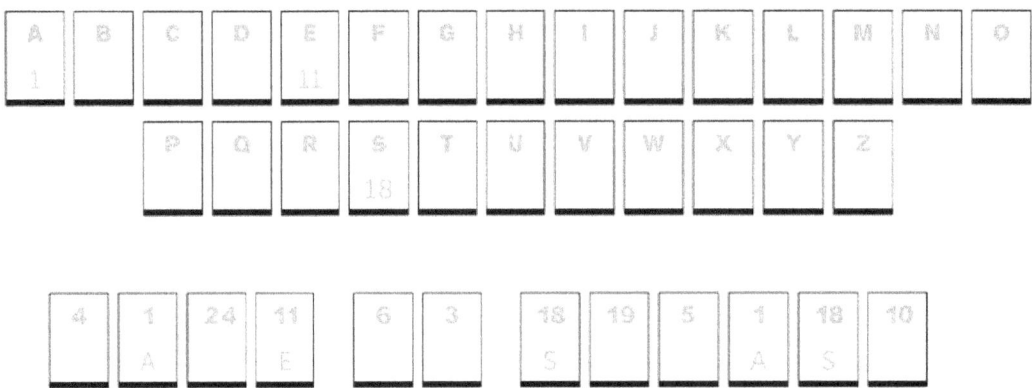

Debra Thomas

Debra Thomas

March 25, 1967 - Present
FIGURE SKATER

LEFT BLANK ON PURPOSE

Debra Thomas

Debra Thomas

Debra Thomas

Debra Thomas

Debra Thomas

Debra Thomas

Directions: read the bio below and answer the following questions.

Hi, my name is Debra Thomas. I was born on March 25, 1967, in Poughkeepsie, NY. I started skating at 5 years. old. I won my first figure skating competition when I was 9. At 10, I began to represent the Los Angeles Figure Skating Club. I placed fifth in the World Championships in 1985 and won gold in 1986. I was 18 when I won the short program and landed four triple jumps to place second in the long program, which was enough to win the overall competition. I also won the U.S. National title in addition to the World Championship that year; these achievements earned me the ABC's Wide World of Sports Athlete of the Year Award that year. I was the first female athlete to win those titles while attending Stanford University full-time since Tenley Albright in the 1950s. I was the first African American to hold U.S. National titles in ladies' singles figure skating. I won the bronze medal and became the first Black athlete to win any medal at the Winter Olympics.

1. How old was I when I won my first competition?
    A. 9
    B. 5
    C. 10
2. I was the first black athlete to win a medal in?
    A. World Championship
    B. U.S. Nationals
    C. Winter Olympics
3. What college did I go to?
    A. Harvard
    B. Yale
    C. Stanford

Directions: Find the words associated with Debra's life and career.

```
L  S  C  G  P  K  F  J  R  K  Q  Y  J  L  V  B  S  V
L  M  V  V  L  A  D  E  M  E  Z  N  O  R  B  F  W  C
W  O  R  L  D  C  H  A  M  P  I  O  N  K  G  B  I  X
G  L  M  C  H  Z  S  M  M  E  G  T  E  M  X  J  T  A
H  E  X  Q  D  R  P  R  T  M  F  A  B  D  Y  B  Z  X
A  N  W  I  N  T  E  R  O  L  Y  M  P  I  C  S  E  E
L  G  S  P  R  F  E  T  L  U  M  X  S  R  A  P  R  T
L  H  I  P  R  E  P  L  A  C  E  M  E  N  T  V  L  G
O  Z  T  O  J  R  O  N  L  K  V  Q  U  O  B  F  A  P
F  J  G  U  M  X  J  X  A  E  S  P  S  A  V  A  N  X
F  Q  B  C  Z  H  R  T  D  I  A  E  E  R  P  Y  D  J
A  C  C  A  R  M  E  N  E  T  C  I  R  H  N  D  L  K
M  N  M  R  O  R  Z  S  M  K  Y  I  H  U  N  K  V  Q
E  B  V  Q  J  K  Y  H  D  U  M  T  S  X  G  F  Z  H
Y  L  Y  Y  P  Y  B  L  L  P  T  G  X  Y  Y  I  S  Z
G  S  B  W  C  N  R  L  O  N  I  D  I  O  H  V  F  T
U  X  F  J  M  S  X  G  G  X  E  O  D  P  E  P  X  O
G  F  G  I  F  E  N  H  D  O  X  W  E  H  Q  R  W  O
```

Find These Words

SWITZERLAND WINTEROLYMPICS FIGURESKATER
GOLDMEDAL WORLDCHAMPION PHYSICIAN
HIPREPLACEMENT BRONZEMEDAL HALLOFFAME
CARMEN

Directions: The images and text form an accomplishment of Debra's. Write the **sentence** below or the right number sequence.

#6

a

 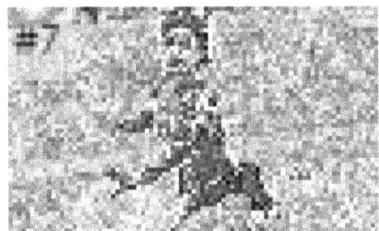

#5 WANTED   #4

to

Directions: Read and answer the questions below. Try and solve the cryptic message. Clue for cryptic message: This is one of Debi's events.

Questions

1) Debi graduated from _____ University.
2) Debi won gold in the short program at the 1986 ____ championships.
3) Debi was the first African American to win the women's _____ at the U.S. Figure Skating Championships.
4) Debi is a member of _____ Kappa Alpha sorority.
5) Debi was the first African American to win a _____ in any sport at the Winter Olympics.
6) Debi ____ as a representative for the U.S. Olympic Committee at the 2002 Winter Olympics
7) In ____ 2005, Debi graduated from the Orthopedic Residency Program at Charles R. Drew University in Los Angeles.
8) Debi is a _____ skater and a medical doctor.
9) Debi made the cover of _____ magazine in 1988.
10) Debi was a practicing orthopedic surgeon specializing in hip and knee_____.

Directions: This is the WGLT Challenge. Solve the cryptogram. As the puzzle solver, you need to find which number belongs to which character. And this can be pretty challenging! You will need to match the number with the letter. There are some letters given to you below. This will help you solve the other words and unlock more characters. **Good Luck.**

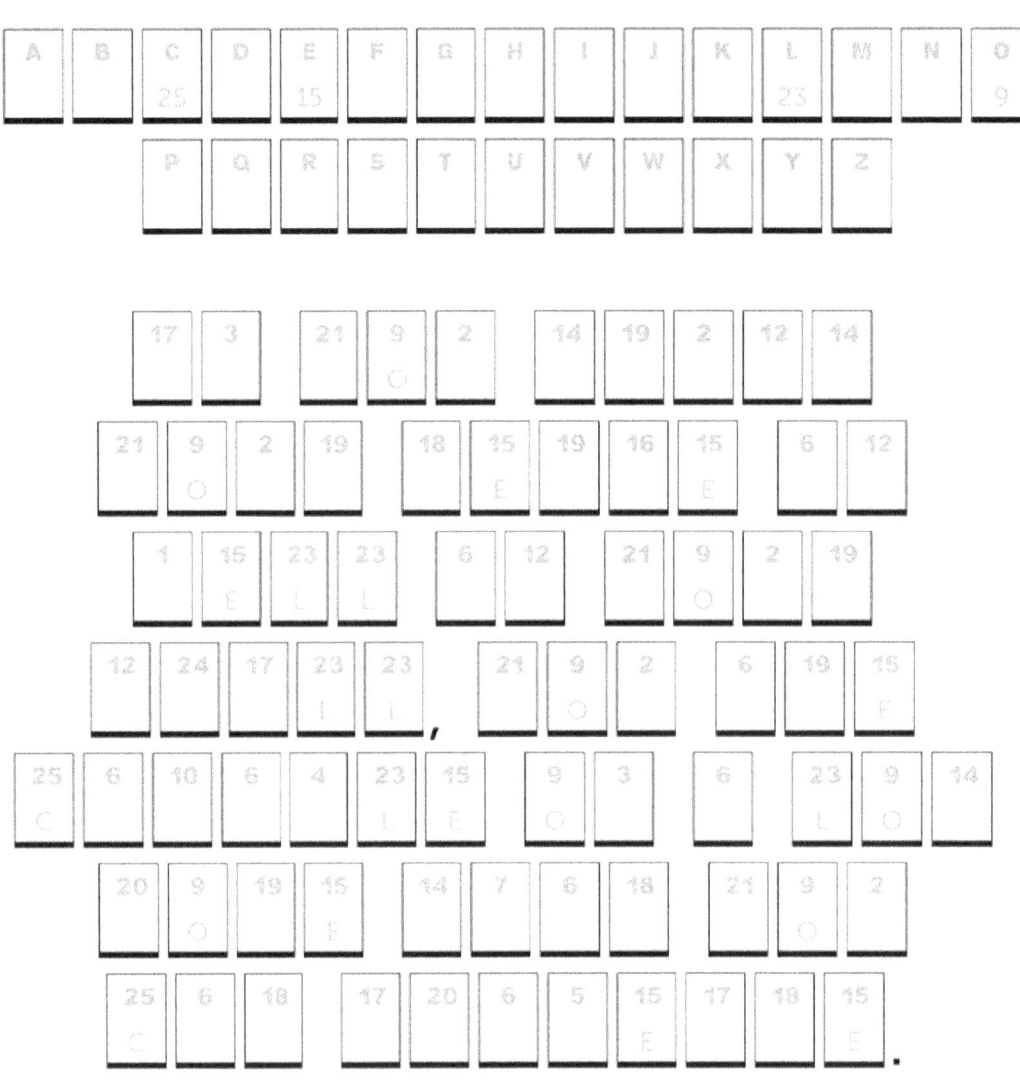

Frank Robinson

Frank Robinson

August 31, 1935 – February 7, 2019
BASEBALL PLAYER/MANAGER

LEFT BLANK ON PURPOSE

Frank Robinson

Frank Robinson

Frank Robinson

Frank Robinson

Frank Robinson

Frank Robinson

Directions: read the bio below and answer the following questions.

Hi, my name is Frank Robinson. I was born on August 31, 1935, in Beaumont, TX. I attended McClymond's High School in Oakland, CA. I played baseball and basketball and Bill Russell was my teammate. I signed with the Cincinnati Reds' minor league team, the Ogden Reds, in 1953. In 1956, I made my major league debut and I tied the then-record of 38 home runs by a rookie and was named Rookie of the Year. My team and I won the National League (NL) pennant in 1961 and I won my first MVP in the NL. I won my second MVP in the American League (AL) in 1966 with the Baltimore Orioles after winning the Triple Crown. We also won the first World Series title in franchise history that year. I'm the only player to be named MVP in both the NL and AL. I helped the Baltimore Orioles win another World Series title in 1970. In 1975, I became the first Black manager in major league history as the Cleveland Indians' player-manager.

1. How many World Series titles do I have?
   A. None
   B. 1
   C. 2
2. What year did I make my debut in the Major Leagues?
   A. 1956
   B. 1953
   C. 1966
3. What NBA player did I play with in High School?
   A. Wilt Chamberlain
   B. Bill Russell
   C. Earl Lloyd

Directions: Answer the questions, to solve the crossword puzzle. You can use the internet if you get stuck on any question.

Across
7) Frank won the _____, Most Valuable Player and the World Series in the same year.
8) Frank is the only player to be named _____ of both the National League (NL) and the American League (AL).

Down
1) Frank was the first black _____ in Major League Baseball history.
2) Frank was ____ into the Baseball Hall of Fame in 1982.
3) Frank helped lead the _____ Orioles to the first two World Series titles in franchise history
4) Frank made his major league debut in 1956 with the _____ Reds.
5) Frank won Rookie of the year while playing in the _____ League.
6) President Bush awarded Frank the Presidential Medal of ____.

Directions: The images and text form an accomplishment of Frank's. Write the **sentence** below or the right number sequence.

#1 the

#7 [crown]

#6 1966

#4 Triple

#3 NOW YOU WON

#5 [motorcycle/race image]

#2 in

1, 3, 2, 4, 5, 6, 7

Directions: Unscramble the words below about Frank. See if you can get the bonus word.

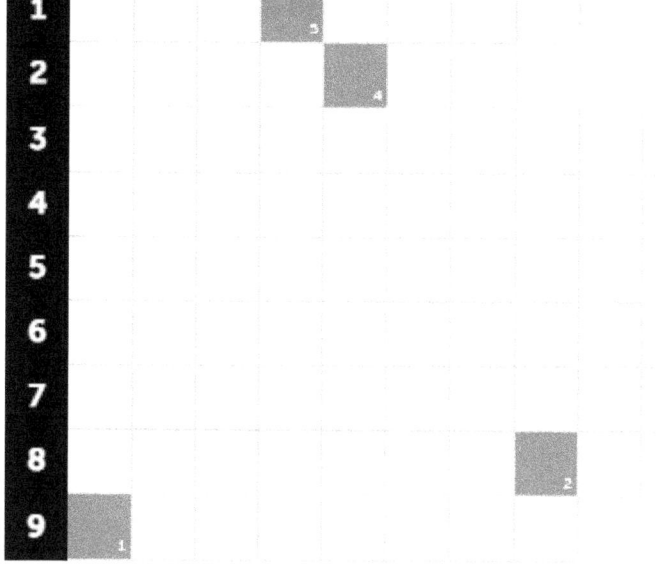

BONUS WORD

| 1 | 2 | 3 | 4 | 5 |

Unscramble Words

1) balblsae
2) naragme
3) inrtpcowerl
4) erlomtareoisbiol
5) rnncnidetcasii
6) alfoaflhme
7) nelaniivcsdledna
8) lpaamvebrsolalteuy
9) n71ej0u9

Directions: This is the WGLT Challenge. Solve the cryptogram. As the puzzle solver, you need to find which number belongs to which character. And this can be pretty challenging! You will need to match the number with the letter. There are some letters given to you below. This will help you solve the other words and unlock more characters. **Good Luck.**

1. What clause stop me for joining the PGA prior to 1960?
   A. Age
   B. Caucasian only
   C. Not good enough
2. What year did I join United Open Association?
   A. 1950
   B. 1948
   C. 1960
3. Who am I known as in golf?
   A. Muhammad Ali
   B. Jackie Robinson
   C. Wilt Chamberlain

Charles Sifford

Answers

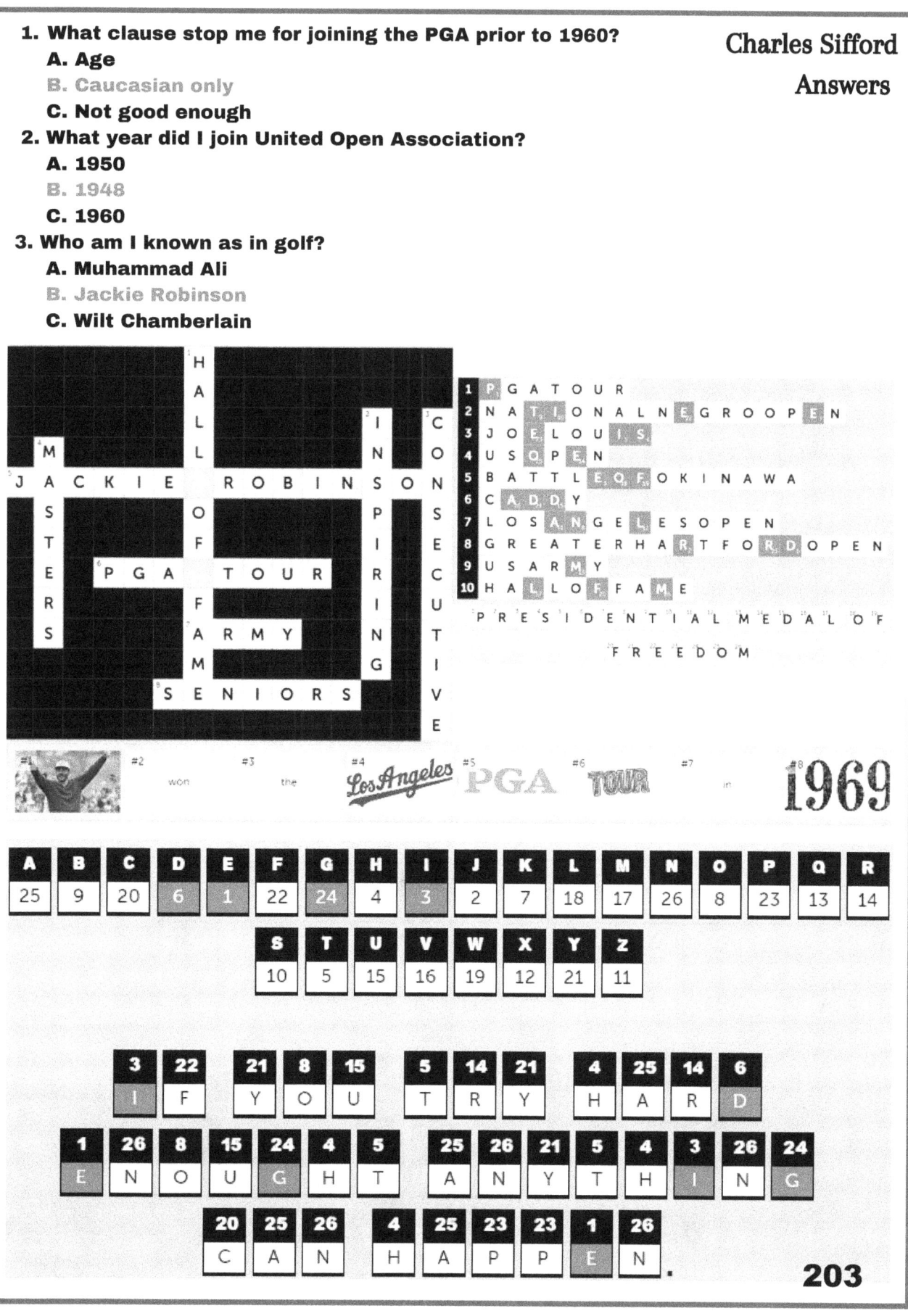

203

1. What college did I go to?
   A. UCLA
   B. Michigan
   C. Duke
2. How many Championships ships did I win?
   A. 5
   B. 6
   C. 3
3. What is my trademark move?
   A. Up and Under
   B. Double Clutch Shot
   C. Skyhook

Ferdinand Alcindor
Answers

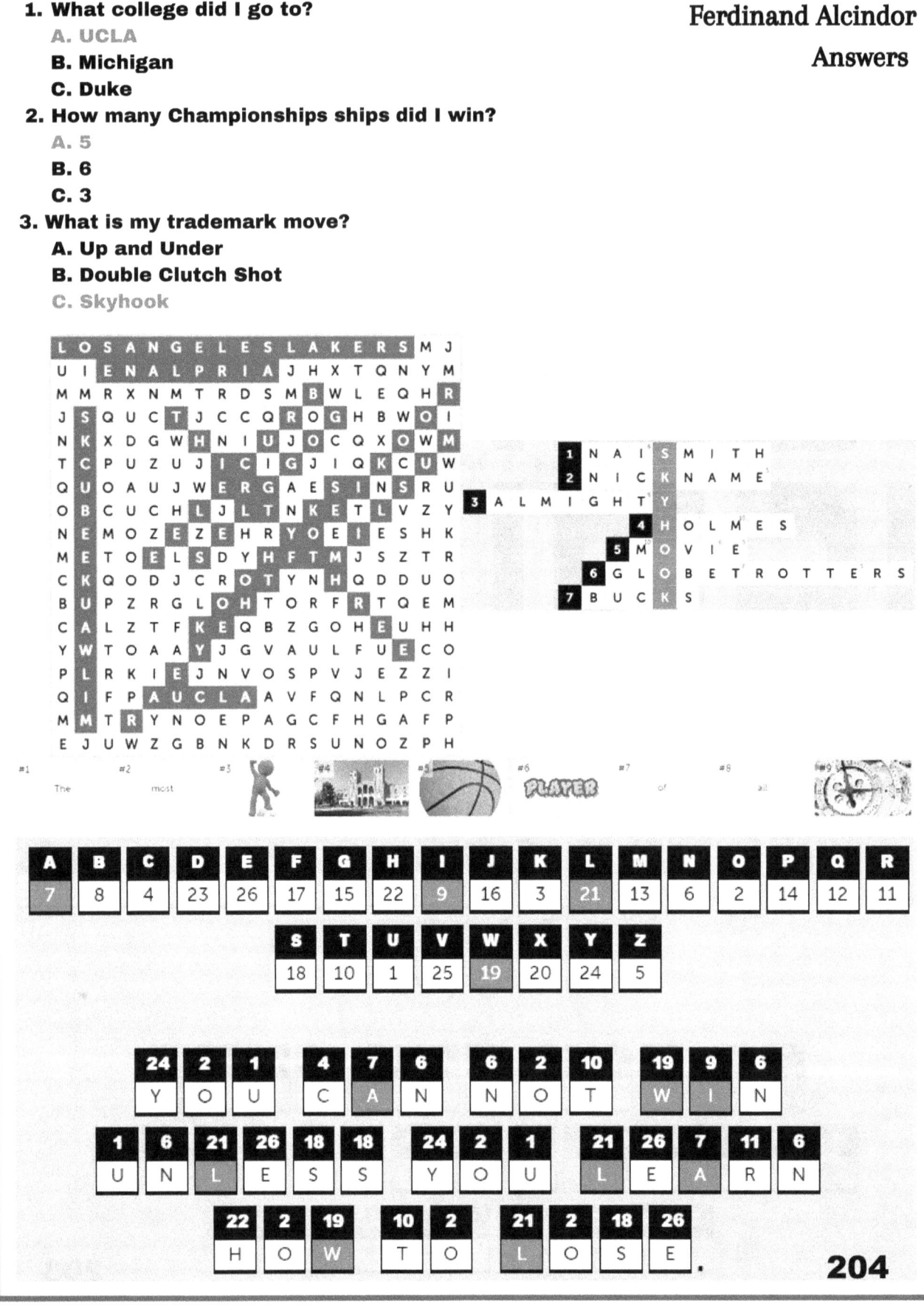

YOU CANNOT WIN UNLESS YOU LEARN HOW TO LOSE.

204

1. Who did I beat to become the Heavyweight Champion?
    A. Joe Frazier
    B. Zbigniew Pietrzykowski
    C. Sonny Liston
2. What year did I become a Pro Boxer?
    A. 1954
    B. 1960
    C. 1963
3. What am I known as?
    A. Baptists
    B. The Greatest
    C. Singer

Cassius Marcellus Clay
Answers

Crossword:
- COLUMBIA
- CHAMP
- VIETNAM
- AFRICA
- THIRTY-SIX
- CASSIUS
- CARTER'S
- DYSLEXIA
- ABOLITIONIST
- SMOKER

Word list:
1. PROFESSIONAL BOXER
2. SPOKEN WORD
3. HEAVYWEIGHT CHAMP
4. SUMMER OLYMPICS
5. ISLAM
6. MALCOLM X
7. LIGHT HEAVYWEIGHT
8. SPOKE WORD

I AM THE GREATEST

#1 The #2 RUMBLE #3 in #4 the #5

Cipher key:
A=10, B=5, C=15, D=6, E=16, F=24, G=22, H=21, I=26, J=14, K=1, L=2, M=13, N=11, O=18, P=8, Q=9, R=7, S=19, T=17, U=4, V=3, W=23, X=12, Y=25, Z=20

IF MY MIND CAN CONCEIVE IT AND MY HEART CAN BELIEVE IT, THEN I CAN ACHIEVE IT.

205

1. What college did I go to?
   A. Tougaloo College
   B. Florida A&M University
   C. Clark University
2. What year did I participate in Nationals?
   A. 1952
   B. 1950
   C. 1949
3. What age did I become NY City Women paddle tennis champ?
   A. 15
   B. 23
   C. 12

Althea Gibson

Answers

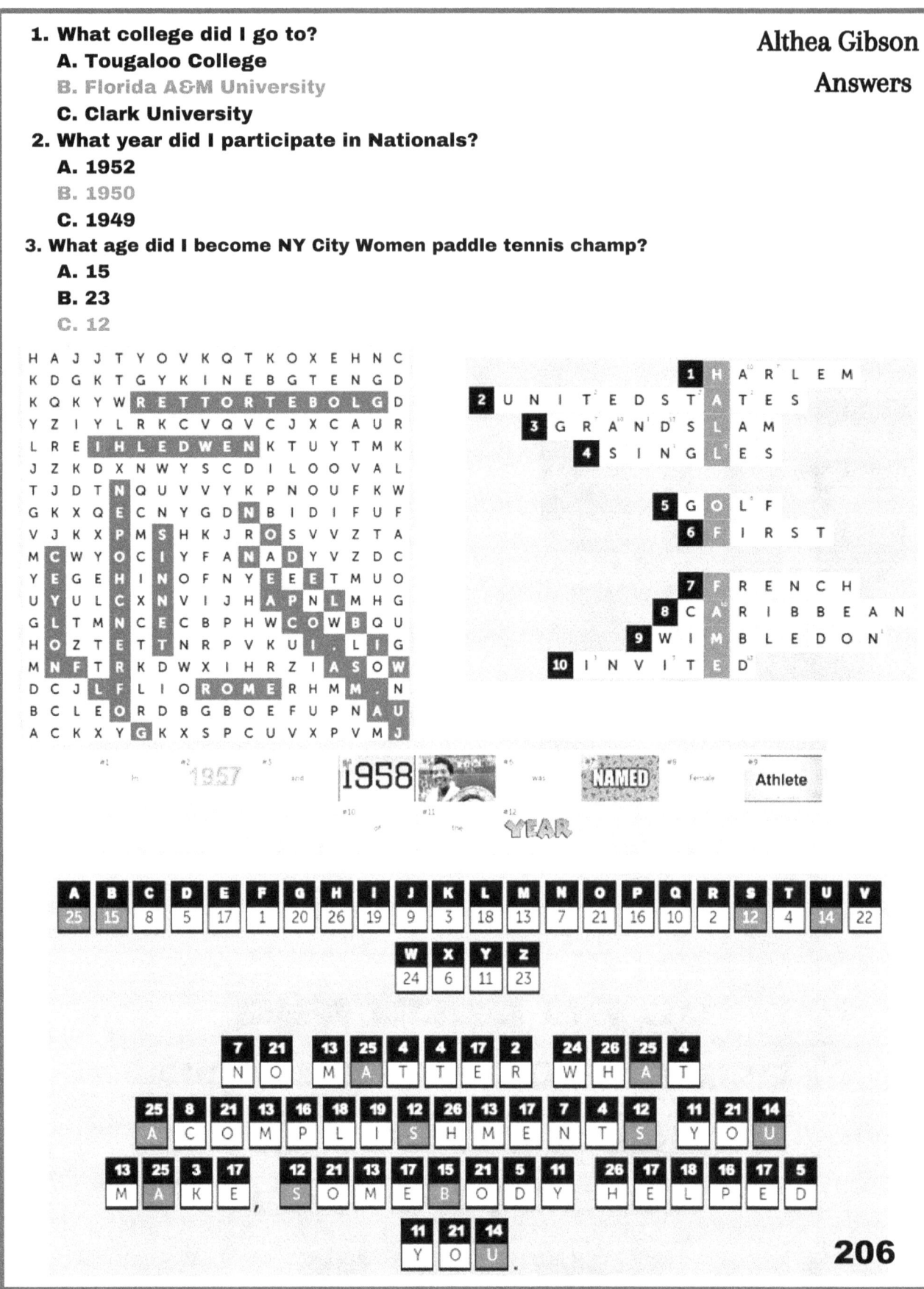

206

Jack Roosevelt Robinson
Answers

1. What sport didn't I play in UCLA?
   A. Track
   B. Lacrosse
   C. Baseball
2. What year did I win my championship with the Dodgers?
   A. 1950
   B. 1955
   C. 1946
3. I was the first athlete to do what at UCLA?
   A. Letter in four sports
   B. Win a championship
   C. Play all year long

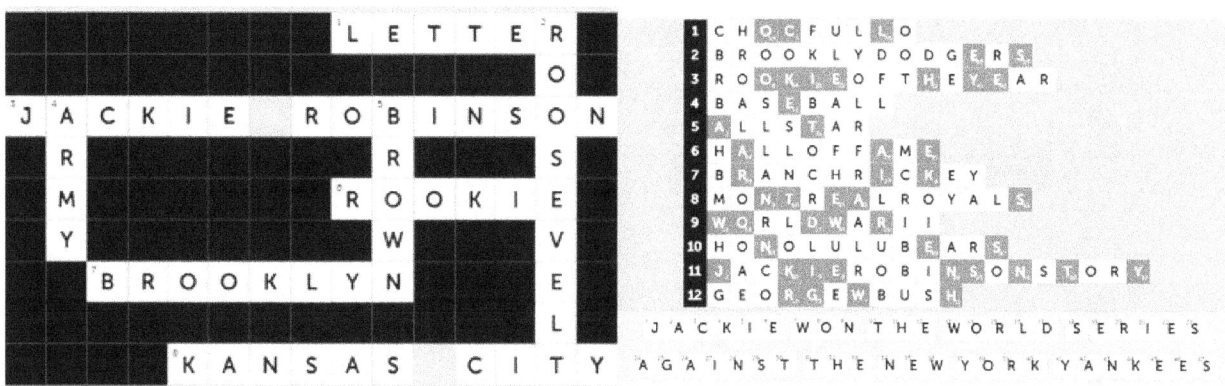

207

1. Who did I get my nickname from?
   A. My mother
   B. My father
   C. My teacher
2. How many gold medals did I win in Summer Olympics?
   A. 1
   B. 3
   C. 4
3. What college did I go to?
   A. The Ohio State University
   B. Michigan University
   C. Alabama University

James Cleveland Owens
Answers

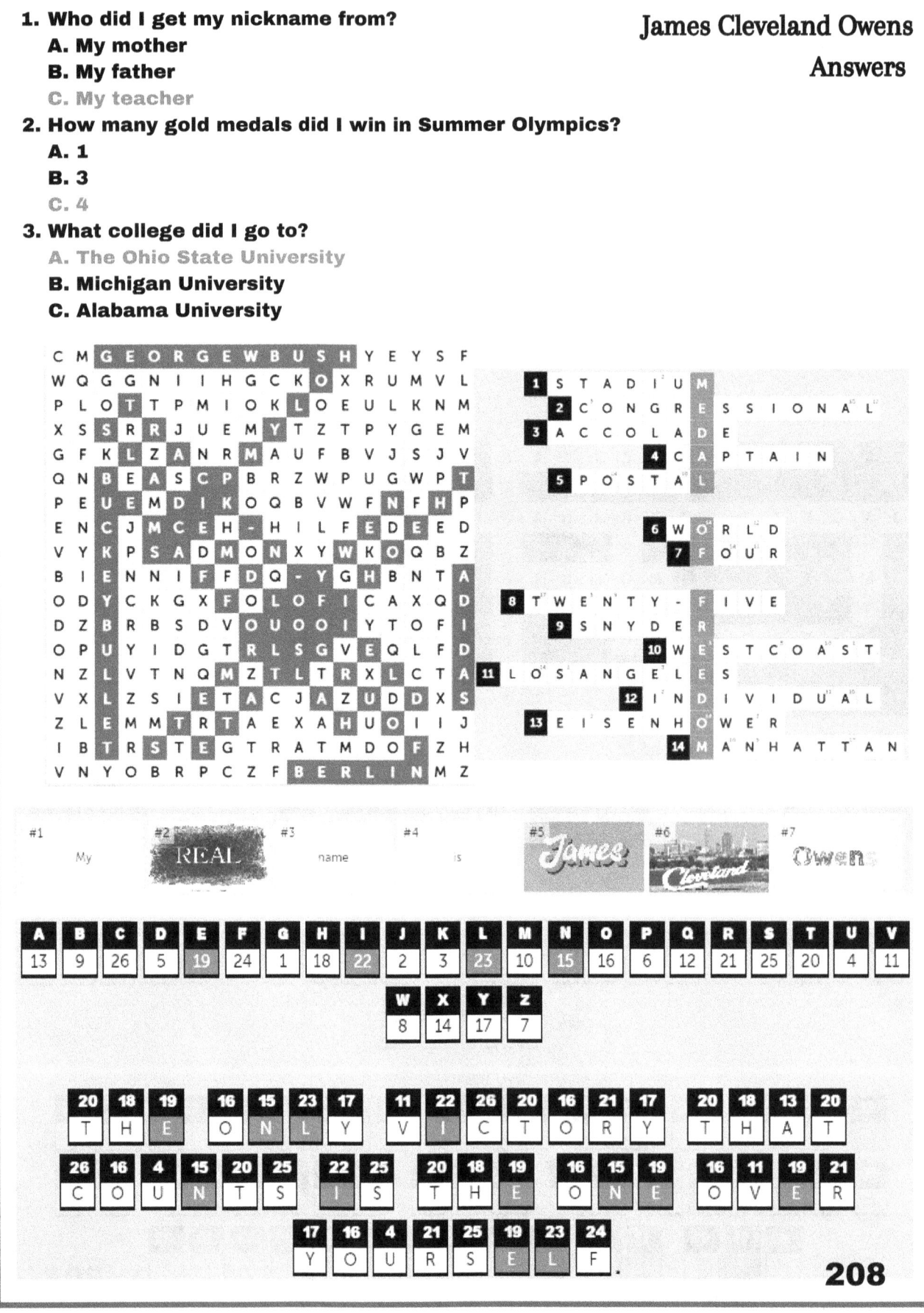

My REAL name is James Cleveland Owens

A	B	C	D	E	F	G	H	I	J	K	L	M	N	O	P	Q	R	S	T	U	V
13	9	26	5	19	24	1	18	22	2	3	23	10	15	16	6	12	21	25	20	4	11

W	X	Y	Z
8	14	17	7

THE ONLY VICTORY THAT COUNTS IS THE ONE OVER YOURSELF.

208

1. How many Grand Slam singles titles did I win?
   A. 1
   B. 3
   C. 5
2. What College did I attend?
   A. Hampton University
   B. Fisk University
   C. UCLA
3. What fraternity am I apart of?
   A. Kappa Alpha Psi
   B. Alpha Phi Alpha
   C. Omega Psi Phi

Arthur Robert Ashe

Answers

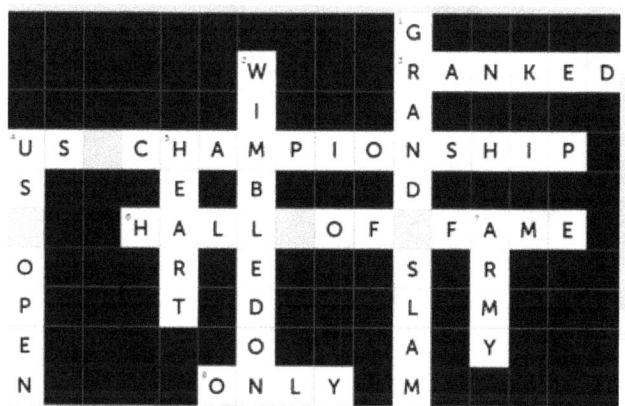
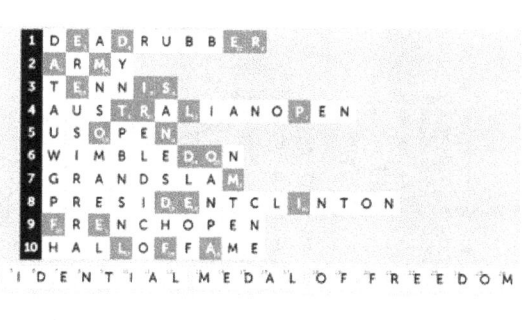

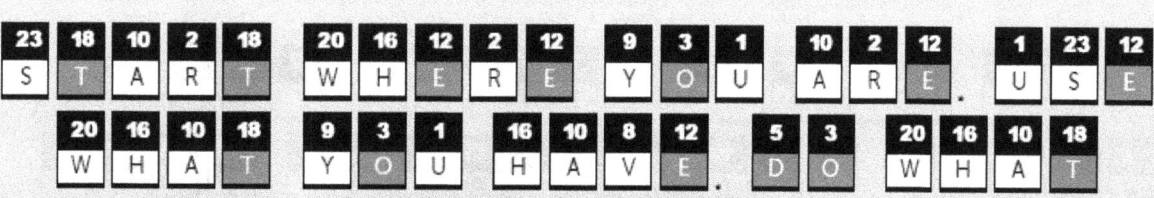

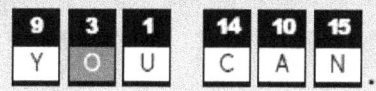

209

Jacqueline Joyner-Kersee
Answers

1. Who was I named after?
   A. My Grandmother
   B. The First Lady
   C. My Mother

2. What year did I set the heptathlon world record?
   A. 1984 Olympics
   B. 1992 Olympics
   C. 1988 Olympics

3. What did I win 2 gold medals in?
   A. Long Jump
   B. 100 meter dash
   C. Heptathlon

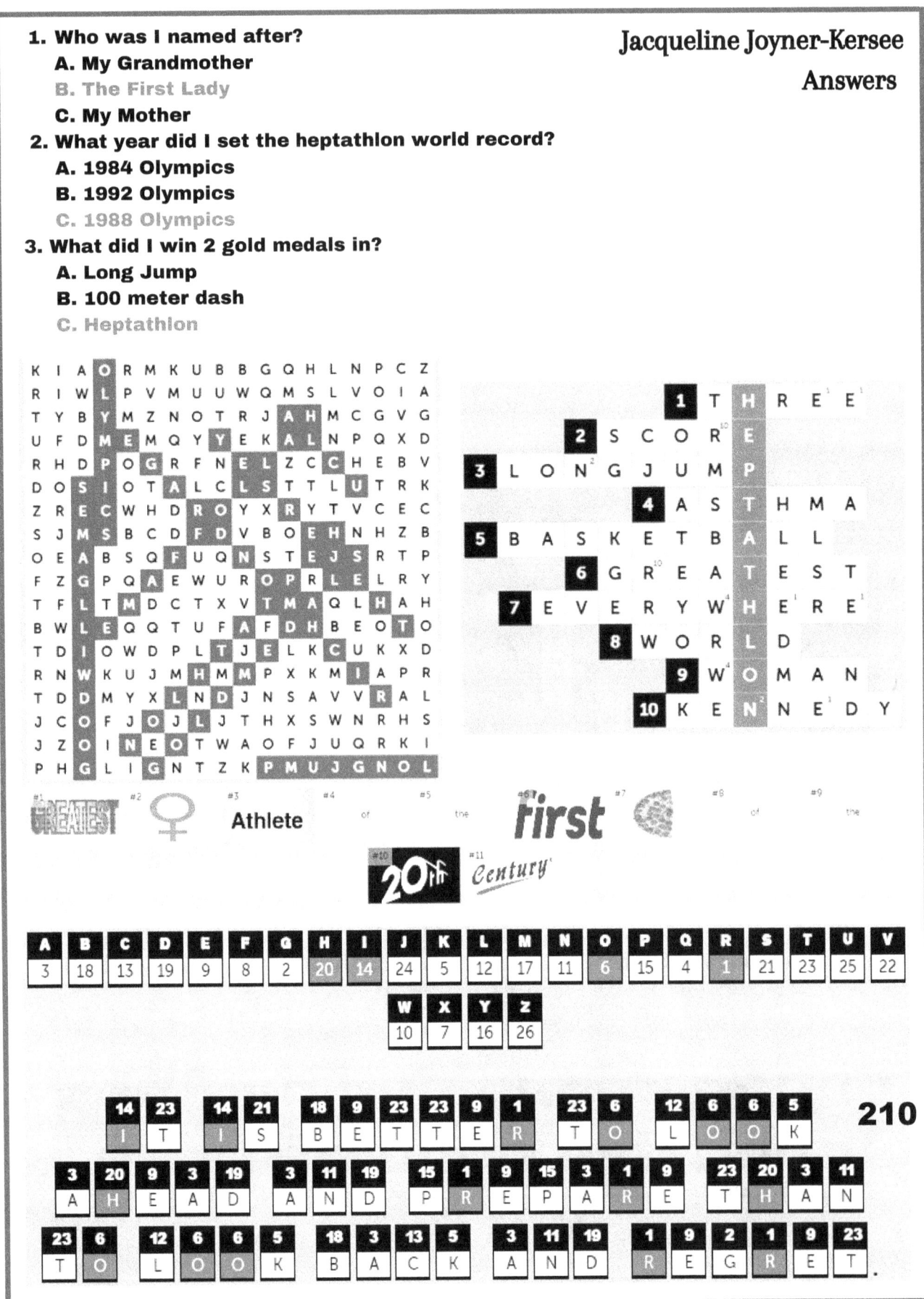

GREATEST ♀ **Athlete** of the **first** 🐆 of the **20th** **Century**

A	B	C	D	E	F	G	H	I	J	K	L	M	N	O	P	Q	R	S	T	U	V
3	18	13	19	9	8	2	20	14	24	5	12	17	11	6	15	4	1	21	23	25	22

W	X	Y	Z
10	7	16	26

"IT IS BETTER TO LOOK AHEAD AND PREPARE THAN TO LOOK BACK AND REGRET."

210

1. What sport didn't I do professionally?
   A. Track & Field
   B. Football
   C. Baseball
2. What year did I win the Heisman?
   A. 1982
   B. 1983
   C. 1985
3. What is my nickname?
   A. The Greatest
   B. BO
   C. The King

Vincent Edward Jackson

Answers

1. HEISMAN TROPHY
2. NIKE
3. LA RAIDERS
4. BASEBALL
5. HALL OF FAME
6. KANSAS CITY ROYALS
7. FOOTBALL
8. BO KNOWS
9. AUBURN
10. CHICAGO WHITE SOX

BO IS SHORT FOR MY NICKNAME
BOAR HOG

A	B	C	D	E	F	G	H	I	J	K	L	M	N	O	P	Q	R	S	T	U	V
15	2	16	4	6	1	21	5	18	26	20	24	12	3	13	11	19	7	23	9	17	14

W	X	Y	Z
22	25	8	10

SET YOUR GOALS HIGH, AND DO NOT STOP TILL YOU GET THERE.

LeBron Raymone James
Answers

1. What team did I play for first?
   A. Miami Heat
   B. Los Angeles Lakers
   C. Cleveland Cavaliers
2. How many teams do I have NBA championships with?
   A. 1
   B. 4
   C. 3
3. What city was I born in?
   A. Youngstown
   B. Akron
   C. Fremont

Crossword:
1. YANKEES
2. PROMISE
3. YOUNGEST
4. GOLD
5. JUNIOR
6. FOOTBALL
7. MAGAZINE
8. HOSTED
9. CHOSENONE

Cipher key:
A=9, B=22, C=8, D=24, E=21, F=7, G=11, H=20, I=25, J=26, K=14, L=12, M=4, N=3, O=19, P=15, Q=16, R=17, S=23, T=1, U=6, V=2, W=18, X=5, Y=10, Z=13

Decoded message:
DO NOT BE AFRAID OF FAILURE. THIS IS THE WAY YOU SUCCEED.

212

Eldrick Tont Woods

Answers

1. How old was I when I won my first event?
   A. 5
   B. 9
   C. 8
2. What year did I turn professional?
   A. 20
   B. 18
   C. 22
3. What college did I go to?
   A. Howard
   B. Fisk
   C. Stanford

Crossword (down):
1. BILL
2. WEEK
3. ELLI
4. AMATEUR
5. BUDDHIST
6. BLUEJEJACK (BLUEJEJ...)

Crossword (across):
- EIGHT
- STANFORD
- GRAND SLAM

Answers list:
1. MASTERS
2. GOLFER
3. TITLEIST
4. NIKE
5. STANFORD UNIVERSITY
6. GOAT
7. PGA TOUR
8. HALL OF FAME
9. WE ARE ONE SPEECH

HOW I PLAY GOLF

#1 _____ #2 is #3 the #4 YOUNGEST #5 PLAYER #6 to #7 WIN #8 the #9 _____

A	B	C	D	E	F	G	H	I	J	K	L	M	N	O	P	Q	R	S	T	U	V
9	1	16	7	11	8	10	13	17	20	21	15	12	23	22	2	18	3	14	4	24	6

W	X	Y	Z
26	25	5	19

THE GREATEST THING ABOUT TOMORROW IS, I WILL BE BETTER THAN I AM TODAY.

213

Serena Williams
Answers

1. What year did I become a professional tennis player?
   A. 1997
   B. 1994
   C. 1995
2. What year did I first obtain the number 1 ranking?
   A. 2002
   B. 2000
   C. 2001
3. How many Grand Slams have I won?
   A. 24
   B. 21
   C. 23

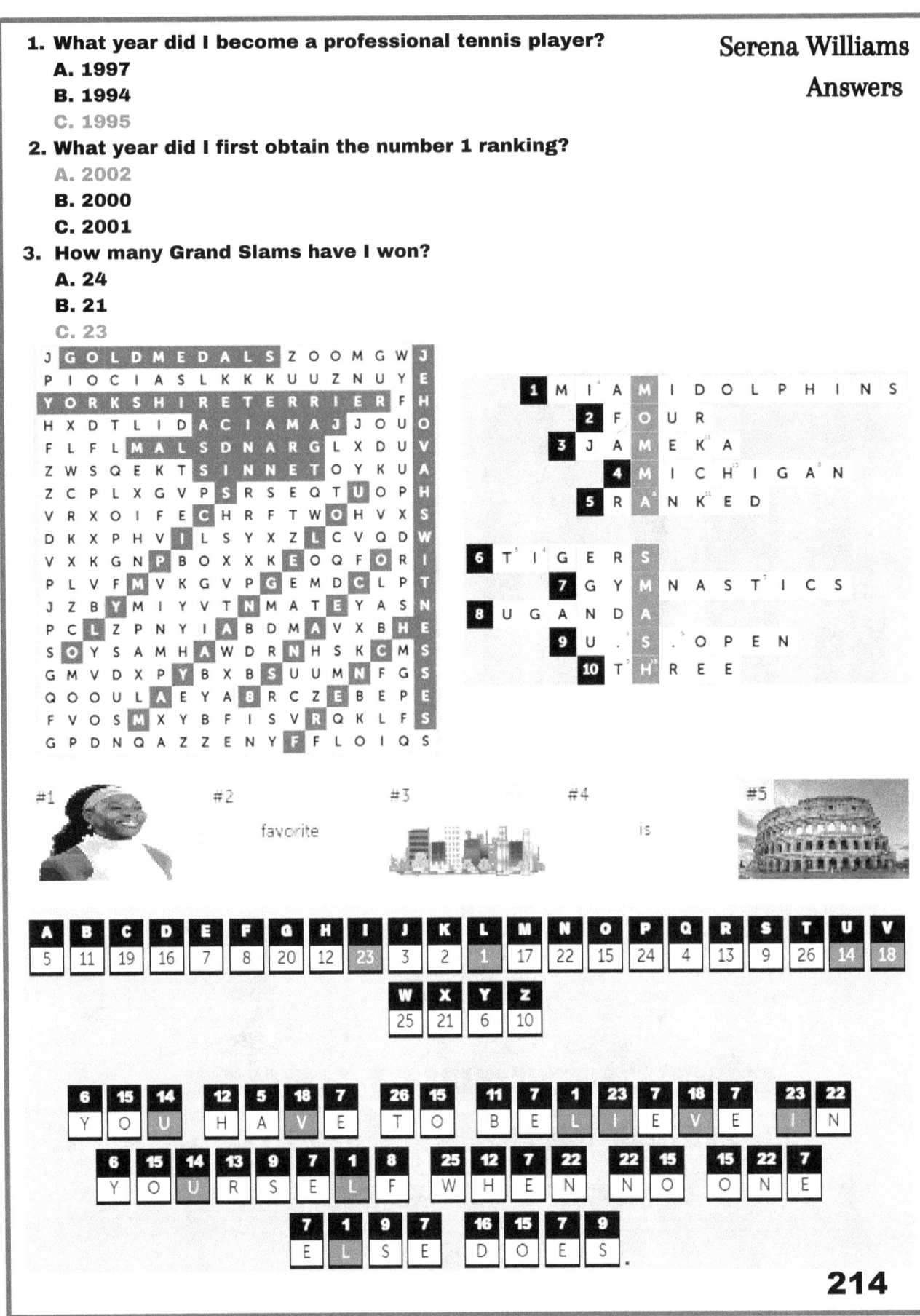

YOU HAVE TO BELIEVE IN YOURSELF WHEN NO ONE ELSE DOES.

214

1. What college did I go to?
   A. Syracuse University
   B. Georgia University
   C. New York Central College
2. What rank was I when I left the Army?
   A. Major
   B. Captain
   C. Lieutenant
3. In my career I averaged ____ yards per game?
   A. 150
   B. 120
   C. 100

James Nathaniel Brown
Answers

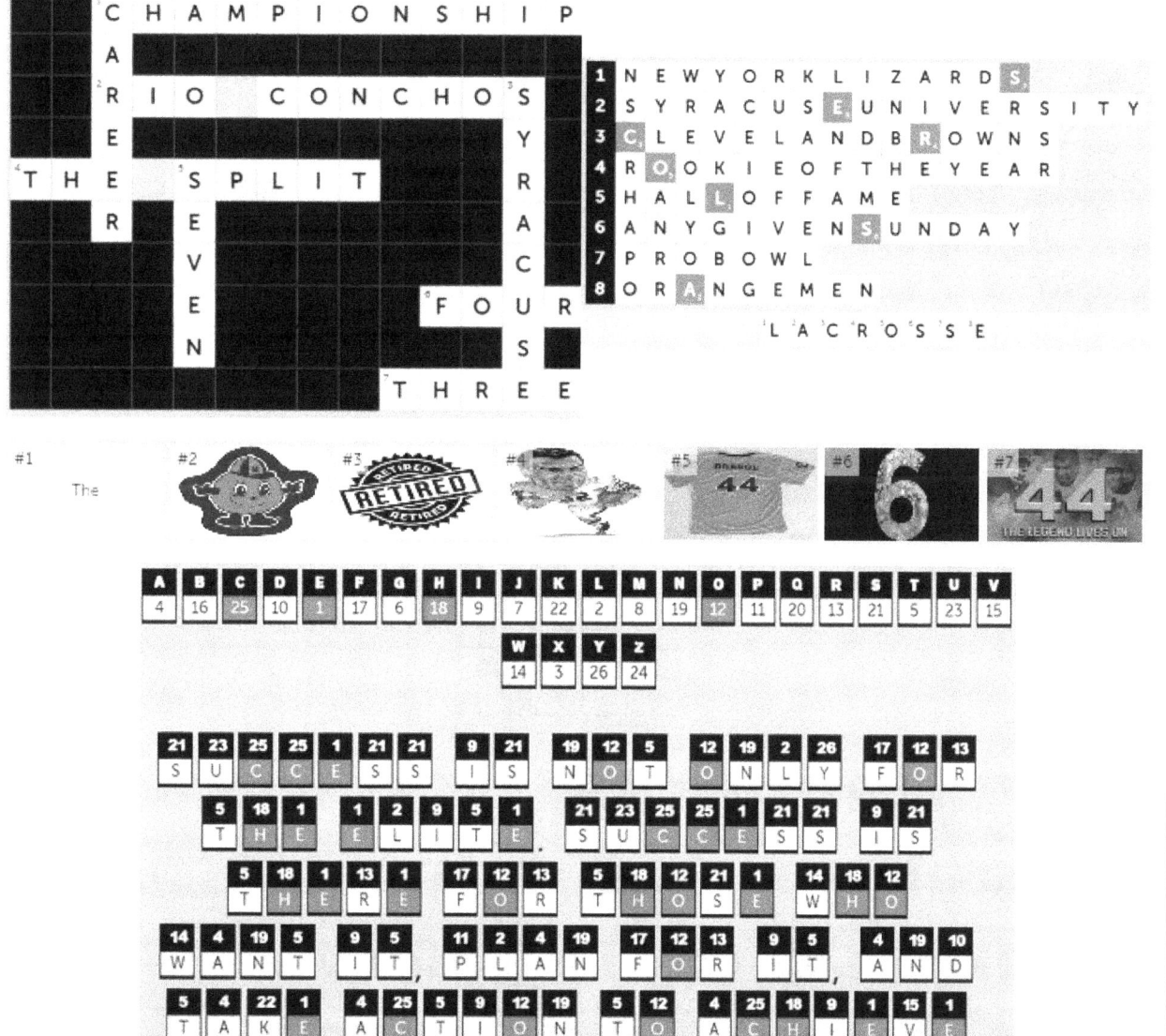

"SUCCESS IS NOT ONLY FOR THE ELITE. SUCCESS IS THERE FOR THOSE WHO WANT IT, PLAN FOR IT, AND TAKE ACTION TO ACHIEVE IT."

Henry Aaron
Answers

1. What semipro team did I play for?
   - **A. Mobile Black Bears**
   - B. Chattanooga Lookouts
   - C. Atlanta Crackers
2. What year did I make my MLB debut?
   - A. 1951
   - B. 1955
   - **C. 1954**
3. What city was I born in?
   - A. Birmingham
   - B. Huntsville
   - **C. Mobile**

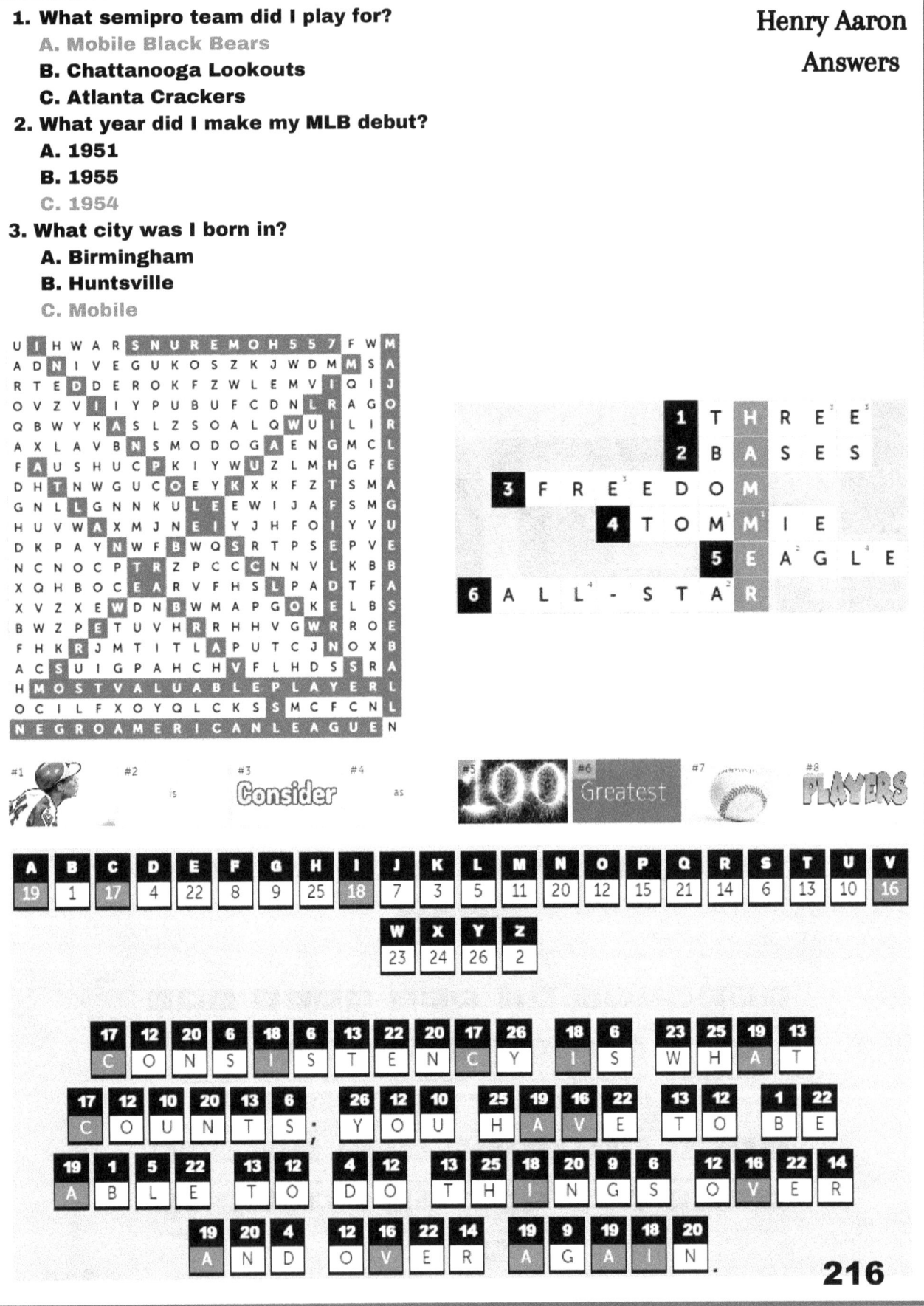

"CONSISTENCY IS WHAT COUNTS; YOU HAVE TO BE ABLE TO DO THINGS OVER AND OVER AGAIN."

216

1. What NBA team drafted me?
   A. Washington Wizards
   B. Portland Trailblazers
   C. Chicago Bulls
2. How many NBA Championships have I won?
   A. 6
   B. 9
   C. 4
3. What shoe line did I start the Jordan brand under?
   A. Reebok
   B. Nike
   C. Puma

Michael Jeffrey Jordan
Answers

```
C H A R L O T T E
A
L         F         T W I C E
L         O         S     O
          R         P     R     B
N O R T H   C A R O L I N A
F         Y         C     N     S
-         -         E     G     E
F         F                     B
A         I         J           A
M         V                 G O L F
E         E         A           L
                    M
```

1 C H A M P I O N S H I P S
2 B A S K E T B A L L
3 N O R T H C A R O L I N A
4 C H A R L O T T E H O R N E T S
5 M O S T V A L U B L E P L A Y E R
6 C H I C A G O B U L L S
7 G R E A T E S T O F A L L T I M E
8 A I R J O R D A N

J U M P M A N

A	B	C	D	E	F	G	H	I	J	K	L	M	N	O	P	Q	R	S	T	U	V
9	3	23	15	17	18	8	5	16	4	10	21	1	20	22	19	26	13	2	11	6	14

W	X	Y	Z
12	7	25	24

I CAN ACCEPT FAILURE,
EVERYONE FAILS AT
SOMETHING BUT I CANNOT
ACCEPT NOT TRYING.

217

1. What college did I go to?
   A. Texas University
   B. Tennessee University
   C. Temple University
2. What Olympics did I win 3 gold medals?
   A. 1956 Summer Olympics
   B. 1964 Summer Olympics
   C. 1960 Summer Olympics
3. How old was I when I won my first Olympic medal?
   A. 19
   B. 17
   C. 15

Wilma Rudolph
Answers

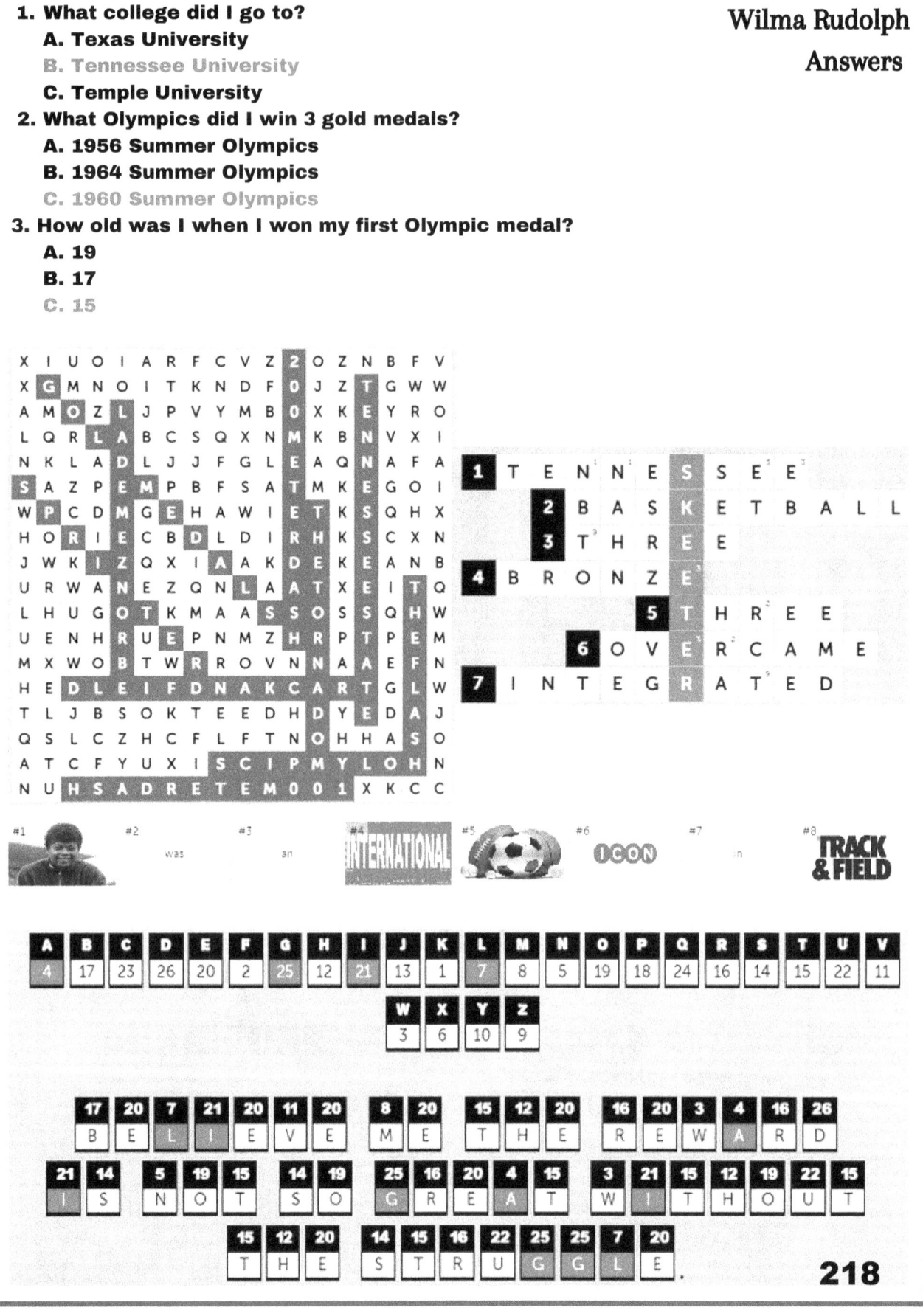

218

Usain St. Leo Bolt
Answers

1. When did I win my first medal?
   A. College
   B. Olympics
   C. High School
2. What year did I first win Olympic gold in 100 and 200 m?
   A. 2004
   B. 2008
   C. 2012
3. What is my nickname from the media?
   A. Black Lightning
   B. Flash
   C. Lightning Bolt

Crossword (Across):
- SPRINTING
- BLUE
- DOUBLE DOUBLE
- NINE

Crossword (Down):
- SCOOBIDOS
- 100
- 200
- PUMA
- METER
- 200 METER

Word list:
1. SPRINTER
2. WORLDRECORDS
3. OLYMPICS
4. VIVATECHNOLOGY
5. ATHLETEOFTHEYEAR
6. CARIFTAGAMES
7. BOLTMOBILITY
8. PUMA

LIGHTNING BOLT

A	B	C	D	E	F	G	H	I	J	K	L	M	N	O	P	Q	R	S	T	U	V
21	16	13	22	9	26	5	8	12	11	18	17	23	14	10	4	19	25	2	15	7	20

W	X	Y	Z
1	6	24	3

THERE ARE BETTER STARTERS THAN ME BUT I'M A STRONG FINISHER.

219

Earl Lloyd Answers

1. What year did I win the NBA Championship?
   A. 1955
   B. 1949
   C. 1960
2. What college did I go to?
   A. Indian University
   B. Virginia University
   C. West Virginia State University
3. What is not my nickname?
   A. The Big Cat
   B. Moon Fixer
   C. The D-Man

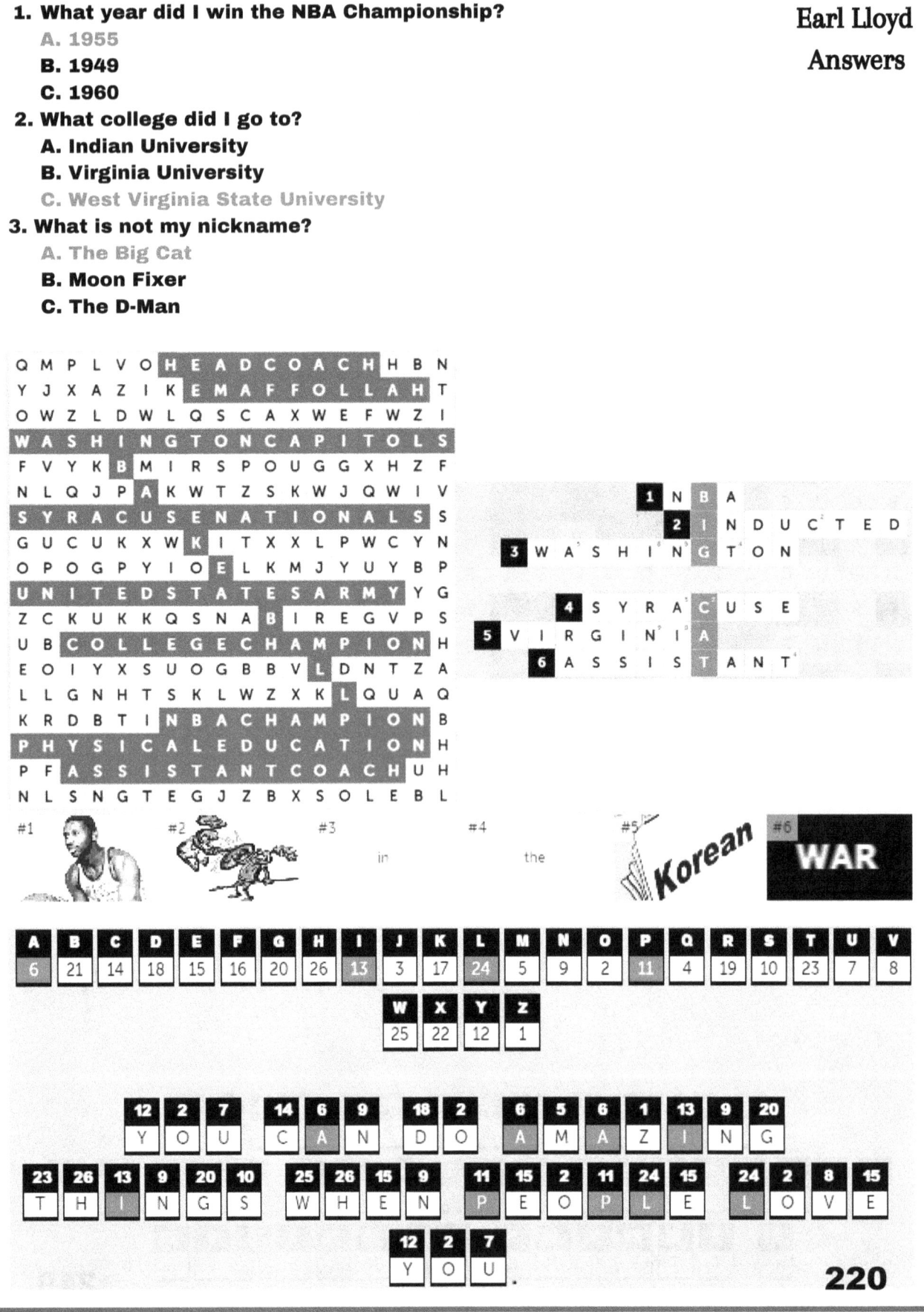

220

1. What position did I play in college football?
   A. Quarterback
   B. Running Back
   C. Defensive Back
2. How many Super Bowls did I win?
   A. 1
   B. 3
   C. 2
3. How old was I when I became an assistant coach ?
   A. 28
   B. 24
   C. 25

Anthony Dungy

Answers

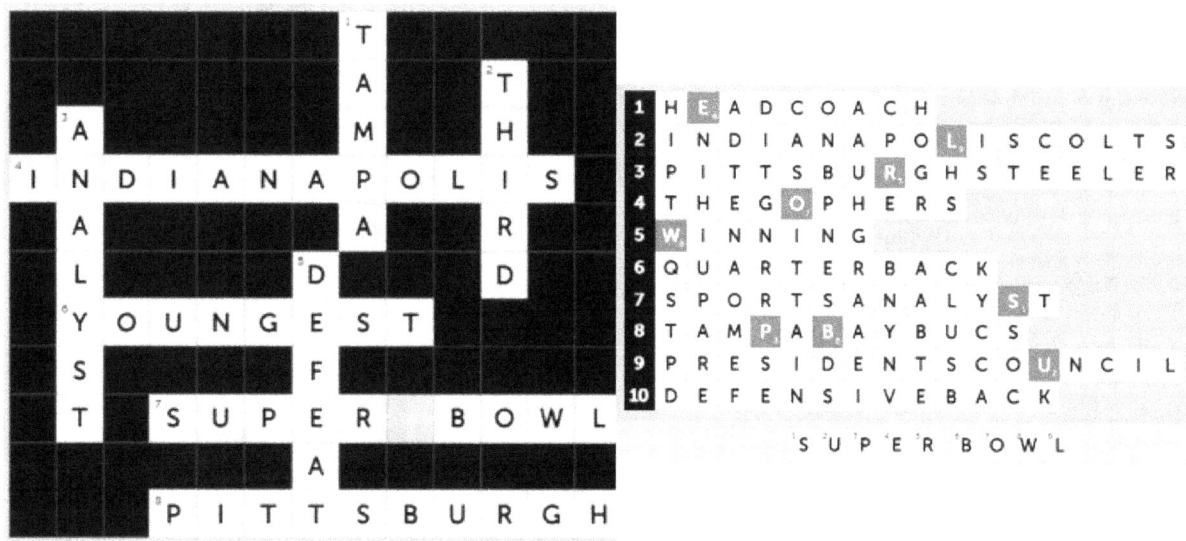

  a  with  the

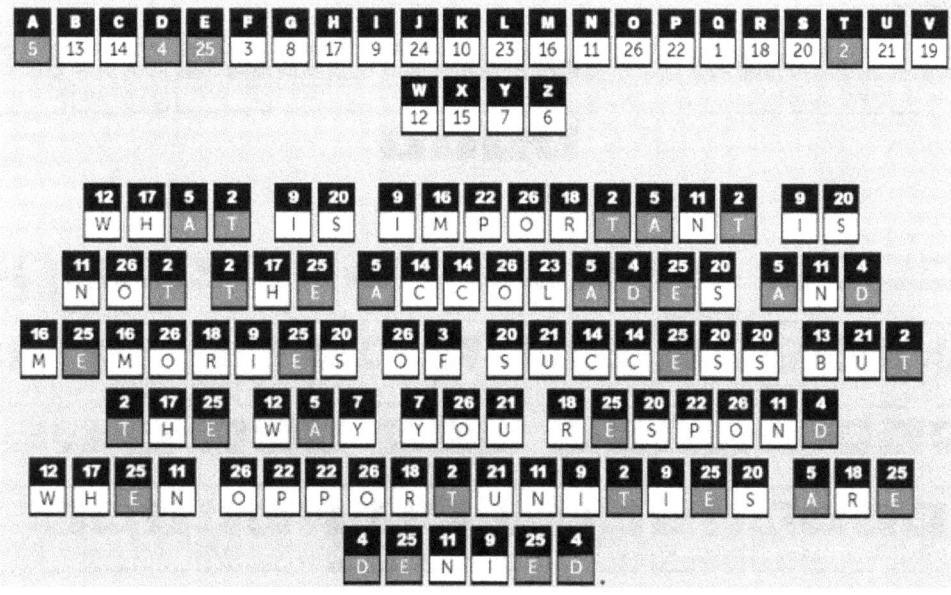

221

1. How old was I when I first dunked?
   A. 15
   B. 18
   C. Never
2. How many WNBA championships have I won?
   A. None
   B. 3
   C. 2
3. What college did I go to?
   A. University of Connecticut
   B. Notre Dame
   C. Tennessee

Candace Parker
Answers

Crossword:
1. ANGEL
2. COVER
3. ROOKIE
4. LEAGUE
5. DUNK
6. ILLINOIS
7. GOLD
8. SPARKS
9. ANALYST

#2 Played #3 for #4 the #5 TENNESSEE #6 Vols

A	B	C	D	E	F	G	H	I	J	K	L	M	N	O	P	Q	R	S	T	U	V
13	15	18	11	8	9	12	4	22	17	1	24	26	5	21	10	20	19	14	25	3	7

W	X	Y	Z
2	16	23	6

TODAY I KNOW THAT THERE IS STILL WORK TO BE DONE, BUT ALONG THE WAY I AM ACHIEVING MY DREAMS.

222

Shani Davis
Answers

1. What was the first year I made the Olympics team?
   A. 2006
   B. 2002
   C. 2004
2. I made what team 3 years in a row?
   A. Olympic Team
   B. World Team
   C. Junior World Team
3. What event did I win my gold medal in?
   A. 500 meter
   B. 1000 meter
   C. 1500 meter

Crossword across/down answers:
- WINTER
- TWO
- OVERALL
- SUCCESSFULLY
- 1000-METER
- THE
- WORD
- SILVER

Word list:
1. SPEEDSKATER
2. OLYMPICS
3. GOLDMEDALS
4. WORLDRECORDHOLDER
5. NORTHERNMICHIGAN
6. VANCOUVER
7. MOSCOW
8. WINTERGAMES
9. COACHING

Cipher key:
A=9, B=19, C=20, D=2, E=16, F=5, G=14, H=26, I=15, J=8, K=11, L=18, M=6, N=1, O=22, P=3, Q=25, R=7, S=13, T=21, U=17, V=4, W=23, X=10, Y=12, Z=24

ANYTHING IS POSSIBLE, BUT NOT UNTIL YOU BELIEVE YOU CAN ACHIEVE IT.

223

Simone Biles
Answers

1. How many World Championship medals have I won?
   A. 25
   B. 19
   C. 32
2. I was the first black gymnast to win this championship?
   A. Olympics
   B. Junior Championships
   C. World All-Around Championships
3. I'm the first woman to successfully land what?
   A. Double back flip
   B. Front double twist
   C. Yurchenko double pike

Word Search (hidden words include: YURCHENKO, GREATEST OF ALL TIME)

Crossword:
1. DECORATED
2. YURCHENKO
3. THREE
4. BLACK
5. NATIONAL
6. OLYMPICS
7. MEDALS
8. PRESIDENTIAL

Cipher Key:
A	B	C	D	E	F	G	H	I	J	K	L	M	N	O	P	Q	R	S	T	U	V	W	X	Y	Z
10	22	8	20	19	26	5	14	7	12	25	9	21	11	17	6	16	3	2	18	24	4	23	13	1	15

Decoded message:

BEFORE YOU CAN ACHIEVE...
YOU MUST BELIEVE IN
YOURSELF. YOU ARE MORE
CAPABLE THAN YOU THINK

224

1. What city was I born in?
   A. Manhattan
   B. New York City
   C. Bronx
2. What year did I sign with Nike?
   A. 2003
   B. 2006
   C. 2008
3. What event did I set a meet record in?
   A. 50 meter
   B. 100 meter
   C. 200 meter

Cullen Jones

Answers

Crossword:
- 1. O
- 2. WORLD RECORD
- OLYMPICS
- 4. GOLD
- 5. UNIVERSITY
- 7. SILVER
- 8. FREESTYLE

Word list:
1. MEDLEY RELAY
2. MAKE A SPLASH TOUR
3. GOLD MEDALS
4. SUMMER OLYMPICS
5. NC STATE UNIVERSITY
6. WORLD RECORD
7. FREESTYLE
8. ESSEX COUNTY

GO WOLFPACK

#1 #2 got #3 a #4 BACHELOR'S #5 #6 in #7 ENGLISH

A	B	C	D	E	F	G	H	I	J	K	L	M	N	O	P	Q	R	S	T
1	8	25	14	11	23	9	10	6	17	24	5	4	12	16	19	13	26	18	3

U	V	W	X	Y	Z
21	2	7	20	15	22

4	1	24	11		6	3		18	19	5	1	18	10
M	A	K	E		I	T		S	P	L	A	S	H

225

1. How old was I when I won my first competition?
   A. 9
   B. 5
   C. 10
2. I was the first black athlete to win a medal in?
   A. World Championship
   B. U.S. Nationals
   C. Winter Olympics
3. What college did I go to?
   A. Harvard
   B. Yale
   C. Stanford

Debra Thomas
Answers

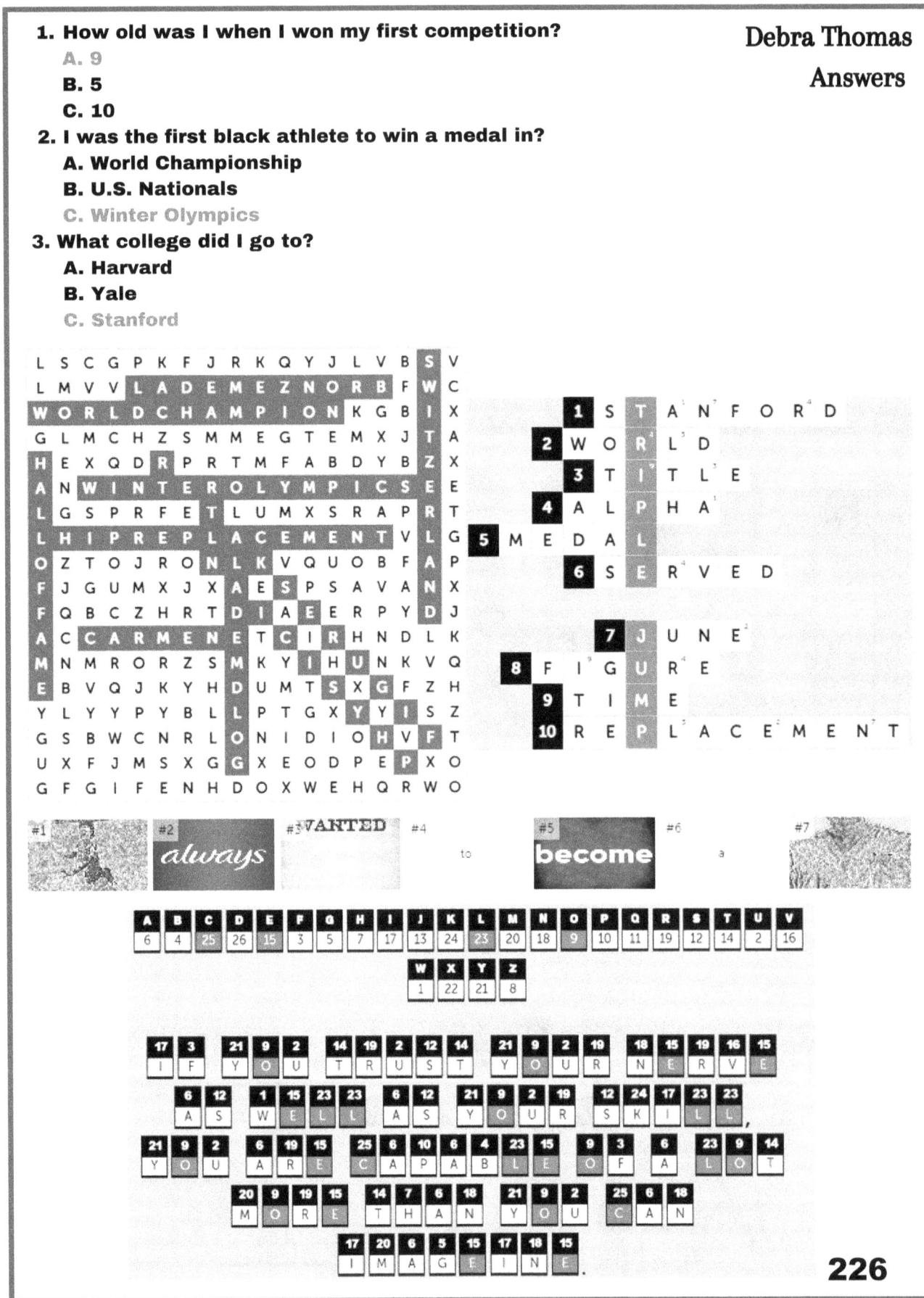

226

1. How many World Series titles do I have?
   A. None
   B. 1
   C. 2
2. What year did I make my debut in the Major Leagues?
   A. 1956
   B. 1953
   C. 1966
3. What NBA player did I play with in High School?
   A. Wilt Chamberlain
   B. Bill Russell
   C. Earl Lloyd

Frank Robinson
Answers

  #3 the  #6 in #7 1966

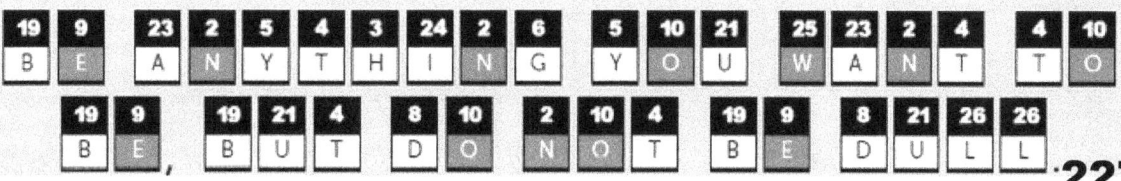

227

This book is dedicated to my grandkids
Anais Isabella Pablo-Antonio
Deyshawn Frank Chambers
Alicia Marie Jackson
Ayianna Marie Chambers
Zion Jamaris Jackson
Jayvon Jerome Jackson

ABOUT THE AUTHOR

Matthew D. Hale, the author of Black Historical Figures is a retired Marine and disabled veteran. He received his Bachelor of Arts in Computer Science from Campbell University and his Master of Science in Computer Engineering from Boston University. Matthew spends his down time making music, traveling, playing, and developing his own video games. Follow Matthew on Facebook/Meta at wegonnalearntoday, Instagram @ w_g_l_t and Tic Tok at wegonnalearntoday. Go to wegonnalearntoday.com or everydollarcountz.com for additional information.

In 2020 Matthew developed an interactive website, www.wegonnalearntoday, to provide access to Black History through games, music and videos. The website grew into the Black Historical Figures workbook series as a way to supplement the black history curricula taught in the school systems.

'In order to grow you must visit uncomfortable places'

10 BOOK SERIES
RELEASE DATES

NOVEMBER 2022

FEBRUARY 2023

MAY 2023

AUGUST 2023

 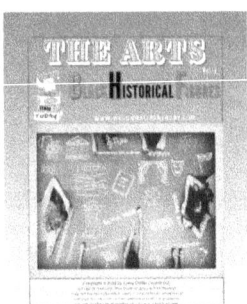

NOVEMBER 2023

GET YOUR COPY TODAY
DON'T FORGET TO TELL A FRIEND

www.ingramcontent.com/pod-product-compliance
Lightning Source LLC
Chambersburg PA
CBHW080335170426
43194CB00014B/2574